Enough Good Men

A WAY OF THINKING

ALBERT BURKE

Enough
Good Men

A WAY OF THINKING

THE WORLD PUBLISHING COMPANY

CLEVELAND AND NEW YORK

PUBLISHED BY The World Publishing Company
2231 WEST 110TH STREET, CLEVELAND 2, OHIO

PUBLISHED SIMULTANEOUSLY IN CANADA BY
NELSON, FOSTER & SCOTT LTD.

LIBRARY OF CONGRESS CATALOG CARD NUMBER: 62-17152

SECOND PRINTING

CONTENTS

CONTENTS

All that is necessary for the forces of
evil to win in the world is that
enough good men do nothing.

EDMUND BURKE

Enough Good Men

A WAY OF THINKING

Cuban Revolution:
The Battle of America

ON JANUARY 8, 1959, Fidel Castro led a band of bearded, ragged guerrillas in cavalcade through the streets of Havana. Flinging his arms wide, white doves perched on his shoulders, Castro told a shouting, weeping crowd of happy Cubans that his revolutionary movement had conquered the dictatorship of General Fulgencio Batista and now would build a new Cuba. That day marked the end of the first phase of the Battle of Cuba, and the beginning of the first phase of the Battle of America. About fifteen months later a force of invaders backed by the United States government was ignominiously defeated in the Bay of Pigs, on Cuba's southern shore, and the Battle of America went into its second phase. Only then did Americans —and even then very few Americans—begin to understand that the Cuban revolution was the beginning of the Battle of America; fewer understood why the battle had begun, and what kind of battle it had become.

The Cuban revolutionaries knew the kind of battle they were fighting. They had never been under any illusions about its importance. One year after the parade through Havana, three months before the fiasco in the Bay of Pigs, Cuba's Number Two leader published a book about the techniques of guerrilla warfare, a specific guide for revolutionaries. It told how to start a revolution with twenty-five or fifty men, and build it until the revolution grew strong enough to topple a government. This man, Ernesto "Che" Guevara, knew exactly what he was talking about. Fidel Castro, Guevara, and the other Cuban revolutionaries had carried out exactly that program, they knew it could be done again. They were already putting the wheels in motion to extend their revolution across Latin America.

The kind of history that these people began writing in Cuba was not intended to stop with victory in Cuba. As the men who led the Cuban revolution see it, there are nineteen more chapters to follow, one for each of the Latin American countries where conditions are ripe for revolution.

As Latin revolutions have gone throughout the world since World War II, the one in Cuba is very special; and for reasons that are mysterious to John Q. American who, without knowing it, is involved in that Cuban revolution. Mr. American doesn't really understand what happened in Cuba from January, 1959, to the spring of 1961. And yet, no other person on this planet has a greater variety of ways to read about, hear about, see about, and know about such things. The tons of newsprint that have passed through his hands; the untold hours of television and radio broadcasts he has seen and heard about turmoil and revolution everywhere around him for years— none of that has prepared Mr. American for today's Cuba.

Mr. American is confused, particularly because, like thousands of other Americans, he has visited Cuba. Many Americans were vacationing in Havana only a few weeks before Fidel Castro made his triumphant entry into the city. But they saw little to suggest that things would go as they have gone in that island country.

The Battle of America began while John Q. American was vacationing in Cuba, swimming in the pool of the Hotel Nacional, drinking daiquiris at the Florida bar, strolling through the velvet evenings, and stopping in night clubs to listen to the hypnotic music of Latin bands. These were not the signs of revolution.

Main Street, Havana, looked just about like Main Street in any large city south of the border. Modern hotels, gambling casinos, exotic restaurants, department stores, and office buildings lined the broad thoroughfares. But those thoroughfares can only be described by the name Tourist Alley. For most American tourists in Cuba, Tourist Alley *was* Cuba; that is, it was the only Cuba they saw. It wasn't Cuba at all, of course, but a transplanted bit of the United States, with its air-conditioned hotels, table linen, and the silver serving dishes in the restaurants. Most of that modern face of Cuba which Americans saw in Havana was, in fact, built by Americans. In Havana's case, much of that transplanted bit of North America was built by a very special group of Americans, who have given many Cuban people a peculiar picture of what life in North America is like just ninety miles away from their shores.

John Q. American had an excellent time in Havana in the fall of 1958, several weeks before Castro reached that city. He lost some money at the gambling tables along Tourist Alley. He did not know that the casinos were operated by American gangsters who also ran most of the bookie operations, dope peddling, numbers and policy rackets, abortion rackets, prostitution, and poker houses in the United States. Mr. American enjoyed the excellent food served in the restaurants along Tourist Alley. He did not know that many of these restaurants were built by the same racketeers with the same racket money. If he lacked feminine companionship, Havana was famous throughout the whole of Latin America for the quality of its

red-light district, conveniently located a few blocks away from
Tourist Alley. And this prostitution was a business enterprise
set up and run by the same racketeers. They shared Cuban
pesos and the American dollars with a number of Cuba's government officials for the privilege of providing this service to
the vacationing public.

All that was part of the transplanted bit of the United
States that made John Q.'s vacation in Cuba a delightful
interlude.

Tourist Alley was not, of course, the only place where American dollars were invested in the Cuban economy, but it was
always the most spectacular part of the Yankee investment
picture there. And there are similar tourist alleys all over Latin
America. For a long time they have been the biggest block to
John Q. American's understanding of what really happens
south of our border, of what life is really like there. John Q.,
you see, is accustomed to the foam rubber mattress and tile
bathroom kind of life. He rarely moves away from this kind of
life, wherever he goes in the world. But there isn't much of that
life in Africa, in Asia, or in South America, except in the
tourist alleys that have been set up to cater to the very few of
the two and three-quarter billion people in our world who
can afford to live that way.

From Tourist Alley it has been hard for Americans to see
the seeds of revolution that have sprouted over much of the
world since the end of World War II, and most recently in
Cuba. Not many Americans are prepared even now to see the
same seeds sprouting over all of Latin America. Castro's right-
hand man, Che Guevara, saw them in Havana, in March, 1960,
more than a year before the battle of the Bay of Pigs, when he
described the Cuban revolution as "Chapter One in the Battle
for America." For the Cuban leaders see those seeds growing
fast in the nineteen other Latin American countries.

What are those conditions? Pope John XXIII put his finger
squarely on the most important of them in his radio message

to Cubans at the First National Catholic Convention in 1959. Five hundred thousand Cubans gathered to hear the Holy Father tell them, "The face of the world could change if true charity were to rule." He meant the charity of the Christian man who knows that it is his duty to give above his own needs to those deprived of the bare necessities of life.

Pope John XXIII was talking to Latins about something they could understand—a face of Latin America which can be seen a short distance from Tourist Alley in any Latin American country. The visitor in Buenos Aires, for example, is always impressed by places like Republic Square, and streets like the Avenue of the Ninth of July. Buenos Aires has some of the best paved, cleanest streets in the world, streets lined with smart shops and hotels. But the visitor to Argentina's capital rarely sees or hears about a place called "The Belt of Misery" which almost entirely surrounds the beautiful part of that city. In this belt, more than a million Argentines live under conditions of filth and poverty which few North Americans alive today have known or can understand. It was from Argentina's belts of misery that the Argentine strong man, Juan Perón, got his support to take over and run that country.

The same belts of misery exist in almost every Latin American city. In the slums of Lima, Peru, ten and twelve people live in one room that has no heat during the cold winter. And in these slums Lima produces one of the highest tuberculosis rates on earth. Brazil's beautiful Rio de Janeiro is surrounded by miserable shacks made from tin cans and packing cases. These conditions are the same in the farming areas of each country too. City or country, in such belts of misery live the bulk of Latin America's people; and they are ready to support anybody who will offer them hope of a better life.

The gulf between rich and poor in every country south of the border is the stuff revolutions are made of. Here I do not mean the palace revolutions that were known in every Latin American country before January, 1959. I mean Fidel

Castro's kind of revolution. As a rebellion, Castro's is not particularly unusual in history; but for Cuba, for Latin America, Castro's revolution has been very unusual indeed, because it is a social revolution, not just a change of political dictators.

Fidel Castro offered Cuba's miserable ones, Cuba's peasants, a better deal, a better life than they had ever known. This group, the *campesinos,* make up half the Cuban population. Castro told the campesinos, in effect, that his revolution would make Pope John's "Christian charity" a reality. This revolution of Castro's was the first revolution in American history to base its policies and its power on the peasant. It was one of the few revolutions in modern Latin American history which was not fought between elite power groups like the military and the upper classes. In all other revolutions, the peasants, the poor, the miserable ones, took no real part. They did not care who won or who lost, because their lives never changed anyway. But Castro told the poor that his revolution was for them; he gave them a sense of political power, and he made them understand what political power meant, and what could be done with it. They flocked to his support, and it is no wonder.

Today the poor, the campesinos, are Castro's main support. Despite crystallized opposition from the upper and middle classes and even from workers in the cities, nearly all the peasants of Cuba are solidly with Castro. They are the backbone of a kind of revolution new to the Western Hemisphere.

This kind of support gives men like Che Guevara the confidence he felt in March, 1959, when he said Cuba had written Chapter One in the revolution of South America. Guevara wasn't just talking. In a visit to Cuba earlier, Jânio Quadros, then a candidate for the presidency of Brazil, said he would follow Castro's example in his country if he were elected. Brazil, he said, had many problems like those in Cuba, problems of corruption, problems of inflation, poverty, illiteracy and disease. Quadros said the need for basic reforms in Brazil was long overdue.

Well, Jânio Quadros won Brazil's presidential election with a landslide majority. His subsequent resignation from the presidency did not indicate any change in the point of view of Quadros or his supporters. The new president, João Goulart, was even more committed to revolution than Quadros. When Quadros resigned, Goulart was traveling in Communist China as a guest of Mao Tse-tung and Chou En-lai. Violent upheaval in Brazil was averted only when Goulart yielded to a demand that the powers of the presidency be cut sharply before he was inaugurated. That postponed the day of reckoning; it did not end it. Brazil, too, is in turmoil. Chapter Two in the Battle of America may be written there, with or without revolution, in South America's largest nation.

But whatever happens in Brazil, or in Cuba; whether Castro stays on, or whether his revolution fails; Cuba and Latin America will never be the same. As Pope John warned, the gulf between the rich and the poor must be bridged. In the continent to the south of us word has gotten around that that gulf can be bridged; that better lives are possible; that schools in which to learn to read and write can be built; that one does not have to age quickly and die young, because of hard work and hunger and disease; that a man may live in a better house than a mud hut, or a packing case with a tin roof.

The trouble is that the word is not being spread by Christian men who practice Christian charity, as Pope John suggested. Instead, the word is being spread by revolutionaries like those who offered jet fighters to Fidel Castro to help him stabilize the revolution in Cuba: the men of the Soviet Union, and later the men of Red China. In addition to building airfields and sending planes, Soviet technicians went to Cuba to build large missile-launching sites which could reach any part of the United States. Soviet and communist Chinese technicians built submarine pens for possible use by their own fleets.

Events such as these are the result of the word spread

around by those non-Christian missionaries. In a period of a few months, sparked by words, there grew up in the Americas a communist-influenced nation which had the power—through its geographical location if nothing else—to pose a military threat to the heart of the United States.

Suddenly, in 1960, a nation which had been an American playground blossomed forth as a threat to American security. The first reports to reach the American public came from men who had been close to Cuban affairs and the revolution, men like Ray Robinson and Neil MacCauley.

Robinson, an American pilot for Cubana Air Lines, told of Soviet MIG planes, missiles, and submarines in Cuba. He had seen the MIGs; he had seen the Russians.

Neil MacCauley, an American who fought for Castro against Batista, was given a farm in Cuba for his services to the revolution. A few months later he left Cuba when he saw the communists take over there. MacCauley began to have doubts when he saw Russians and Chinese communists, and Czechs, and Poles, and Hungarians, and Yugoslavs in Cuba. The Russians were the most conspicuous because they always traveled in groups of three or four, and they did not mix with the people at all.

I asked MacCauley what he thought these people were doing in Cuba. Did he think they were just agricultural technicians, or did he think they had more important duties?

MacCauley was certain that secret police and intelligence agents were mixed with this group, and he was sure that there were political organizers too.

Ray Robinson and Neil MacCauley were among the first Americans to realize that the problem posed by Cuba was serious, that Cuba had become a communist-controlled base in the Americas, and that it could become a direct military threat to American homes, American factories, and to the American future.

This is the obvious thing that concerns and disturbs most

Americans: Cuba as a military threat in an age when inter-continental ballistic missiles can travel across continents and oceans. Today missile-carrying nuclear submarines are operational parts of the U.S.S.R.'s submarine fleet as well as our own, and the Soviet Union and communist China are aware of the enormous importance of the sub as a missile-launching platform. That is why—although most of us still do not realize it—the military threat posed by Cuba is not the most important threat to America. No base on land, whether it is in Cuba or any other place, can compare with the atomic submarine in modern warfare. This does not mean that military bases on land have no value, but it does mean that Cuba is not primarily important to a communist Russia or to a communist China as a military base.

The leaders of the two communist powers have other bigger and more important goals in Latin America than gaining a military foothold in our front yard. Cuba is particularly important to the Soviet Union and to communist China in ways that most of us know little or nothing about. It is hard for Americans to see the kind of person who has become the backbone of a revolutionary, communist power in Cuba from the tourist alleys south of the border. Those farming people—poor mestizos and Indians for the most part—do not frequent the hotels, the bars, the restaurants, or gambling casinos where Americans spend too much of their time. But it is that kind of person and his reason for backing the kind of revolution that was accomplished in Cuba in 1959 that makes that island country particularly important to a communist China and the Soviet Union.

What is there about the revolutionaries and the revolution in Cuba that is so special? The root of the answer lies ignored in relatively recent history.

When Lenin, the father of Bolshevism, tried to make revolution work in Russia, he had to face a grave problem. His followers had taken over the Russian revolution in order to set

up the world's first communist state. Lenin's problem was
that Russia was alone when theoretically she was not supposed to have been alone. Russia was supposed to have been
only one of many states that were to explode in revolution
after the First World War, according to communist theory.
There was supposed to have been a rising of workers and peasants all over the world that would have led quickly to a communist world. But this did not happen. When he saw that it
would not happen, Lenin is supposed to have decided that the
best way to bring about a communist world would be by con-
centrating not on revolutions in advanced industrial nations,
but by working for revolutions in their colonies and what were
called the spheres of influence of the empire powers: Britain,
France, Belgium, Portugal, Spain, the Netherlands. Lenin is
supposed to have phrased that decision in these words: "The
way to victory for communism in the west lies by way of
Peking and Calcutta."

Experts on Soviet affairs have never been able to agree on
the origin of this statement. Some say Lenin did make it and
some say he did not make it. But this does not really matter,
because another Soviet leader did say much the same thing
later. Shortly before he died in 1953, Joseph Stalin said that
the way to world victory for communism lay in an alliance between the Soviet Union's interests and those of the former
colonial and oppressed peoples of the world. Both statements
lead straight out of the past to history made by the communists since the end of World War II.

Those statements also lead from Moscow to the Cubans
who, by Fidel Castro's own definition, were among the world's
colonially oppressed peoples. According to Castro, Cuba was
first oppressed by Spain in the early 1500s. The Spanish-Ameri-
can War put an end to Spanish colonial rule over the island,
but after 1898, Cuba became what amounted to a colony of
the United States. According to Castro, this situation lasted

until January 8, 1959, when he entered Havana determined to make Cuba free from North American oppression.

This may not be history as we learned it from our American history books, but it is the kind of history Castro and his followers believe. It is the history now being taught in Cuba's primary and secondary schools.

It was a kind of history the Cuban campesinos believed, and wanted to end. Take the story of Juan Ibarra, for example. He had one ambition when he joined Castro in 1956: to see Cuba free. Juan Ibarra wanted freedom from a government and a way of life that allowed "foreign interests" and "big landowners" to take farm lands away from Cuban farmers to be worked for the benefit of people outside Cuba. He had in mind particularly seven companies owning a total of five million acres of Cuban farm land—half the land under cultivation in all Cuba. This land produced agricultural products that few Cubans used, and profits that few Cubans saw. The home offices of the seven companies were located in the United States. The work of Cubans on those five million acres paid dividends to American investors; not to Cubans. Ibarra called this colonialism, and he fought for what he called freedom and for land reform in a nation where most of the people farm.

Juan Ibarra had worked for several years as a mechanic at Guantánamo Naval Base, the American installation in eastern Cuba. Before that, Ibarra grew up as one of eight children born to peasants who owned no land, who earned their living cutting sugar cane for one of the one hundred and sixty-one sugar grinding mills on the island. Until he was fifteen years old the world of Juan Ibarra reached from his home to the general store in the nearby village. His home was a squat, windowless, airless shack made of leftover palm tree lumber. Shacks like these were home to hundreds of thousands of Cuban peasants who lived and worked their lives away under conditions that were once the rule in Europe—but a thousand years ago.

Under these primitive farming conditions, the peasants aged fast and died young. Juan was fifteen years old when his father died at the ripe old age of thirty-six. His father was helped to an early death by a variety of infectious diseases that still affect most Cubans who live outside the cities. There were health services in Cuba before Castro. Health services in the cities were excellent, but they did not reach down to the level of the campesino and his family.

Hunger, however, did reach down to their level. Juan knew hunger every day of his life, even when both of his parents worked during the sugar time. Each year, during the long off-sugar season, when there was no other work to be had, conditions became desperate for these people. So Juan Ibarra joined Fidel Castro in 1956, nursing his burning ambition. Is it still hard to understand why he wanted to see Cuba free, free of governments which did little or nothing for the bulk of Cuba's people, the farming peasants, and kept them out of the Twentieth Century?

Juan developed his burning ambition while he worked at the American naval base. Guantánamo Bay, like Tourist Alley in Havana, is another transplanted bit of the United States. At Guantánamo, Juan saw the Twentieth Century up close. He saw decent housing, good schools, medical care and good wages. He heard all about the "good life" on the base radio, he saw evidence of that life in American motion pictures and on television. He was converted by these sights. Juan took to the hills with Castro, to help bring about what he called "economic reform." What he meant was that he wanted to bring to Cuba an economy that spelled the good life. This meant Juan wanted industrial development for Cuba. It meant a drastic overhaul of Cuba's farming system, which kept the people back in the Middle Ages. Juan had no idea how this could be done; he only knew that it had to be done. His stay among the Americans had made a revolutionary of Juan Ibarra.

José Martinez, another kind of Cuban worker, agreed with Juan about the need for revolution. José also joined Castro in 1956 because José also had a burning ambition. José's ambition was to see Cuba free of a way of life that allowed foreign interests to dig and haul ore out of Cuban mines. The ores were manganese, cobalt, and nickel. José was a miner, and although he received good wages working for a Cuban branch of a North American company he resented the fact that Cuba's mineral riches were not being worked in Cuba to make more jobs and better lives possible for his people. He resented the fact that for years Cuban iron ore had been shipped to Bethlehem Steel Company plants in Baltimore, Maryland. Cuban ores created more jobs and better lives for Americans there. José Martinez wanted to see economic reform in Cuba too, the kind that would force foreign users of Cuban minerals and ores both to mine them and process them in his country. As José understood Cuban history, ever since the year 1511, foreigners, first Spain then the United States, had been robbing Cuba of her minerals and ores; so José and Juan fought their way into Havana with Castro to change that.

This desire for change involved many other Cubans. There was Pedro Jiminez also. Pedro's interest in change was not quite the same as the others; his burning ambition was to see Cubans treated as dignified human beings. From Indonesia, on the other side of the world, through mainland China, into and across Southeast Asia, into the Middle East and into Africa and to Cuba, since the end of World War II, Western Europeans have been pushed out by non-European peoples. At the heart of this kind of history, written over the past fifteen years, has been a reaction, a revulsion, against the European idea that somehow men with light-colored skins were better human beings than men with dark-colored skins.

Only a few years ago, Europeans with light-colored skins wrote and talked about the dark-skinned peoples as though they were "the white man's burden." The whites did this while they carved the world into empires and spheres of influence. In their behalf, let it be noted that Europeans were not the first people in human history to believe this kind of nonsense. In other times, as now, this racial bunk fell apart. Today, there is no subject about which practically all the world's people are more sensitive.

Pedro Jiminez of Cuba is sensitive about racial prejudice; and sensitive people like Pedro, and Juan, and José have changed the whole political map of the world since 1945, in revolutions which have just about wiped out the European empires and their spheres of influence. People like Pedro, and Juan, and José have made Cuba particularly important to the communist East Europeans and to the communist Chinese, and particularly friendly toward those communist lands which are "officially" free from race prejudice. The kind of world these Cubans live in is desperately in need of reforms: Juan's land reform, José's economic reforms, and Pedro's social reforms. Cuba and the other lands must have industrial development to change their world from the poor, agricultural place that it is, to the better, more industrialized place that it might be. This is what Juan, José, and Pedro fought for in Cuba, and this is just the sort of interest that Joseph Stalin said the Soviet Union should support in order to bring about a final victory for communism over the non-communist West. There is a direct line from the theories of Lenin, and the actions of Stalin, to Fidel Castro's revolutionaries Juan, José, and Pedro.

Because John Q. American does not live in the same kind of world with Juan, José, and Pedro, he did not see the kind of Cuba that those men fought to change. He doesn't understand the serious threat to his way of life that these Cubans have helped create. Somehow, in the tons of newsprint that John Q. American has read, and in the uncounted hours he has spent watching and listening to television and radio, there has been little to help him know how and why the phrase "land reform" is the stuff of which revolutions are made. He has not learned that he is really not a better human being than Juan, José, and Pedro—but mainly a luckier one, for the time being. This trouble for John Q. American lies in his misunderstanding of Cubans, Indians, Chinese, and Africans, among others. After all, when he compares his kind of life with theirs, he asks: If those people had minds that were just as good as ours, and if they could do things just as well as we can, then why aren't they living as well?

John Q. American's newspapers, and radio, and television have not helped him to know much about the kind of world in which he lives, especially how and why he has been able to live so much better than Cubans, Indians, Chinese and Africans. An incredible charge? This can be made clear by his reaction, or lack of reaction, to an incident reported in the press late in 1959.

One night John Q. American settled down with his favorite newspaper to catch up with what was going on in the world. A lead article on the front page discussed an argument in progress in Congress about the Pentagon. An Air Force general was complaining about not getting enough money to keep up a round-the-clock-in-the-air alert of nuclear bomb-carrying planes of the Strategic Air Command. John Q. read through this lead story, but he wasn't particularly concerned about it. He felt that on the ground or in the air, the important thing was that we had those jet-powered bombers in the Strategic Air Command. Wherever trouble might develop—whether in Cuba or Timbuktu—those planes were ready to protect him. John Q. went on to the rest of his newspaper.

On an inside page his eye caught a small news item from a place called Port Nickel, Louisiana, about a factory which cost forty-five million dollars, but which was not producing anything. It was gathering dust and cobwebs because Castro had interfered with the export of minerals. John Q.'s eye caught the words "nickel" and "cobalt" and passed on to more interesting matters of the moment. Five minutes later he had forgotten all about it, not realizing that the full measure of the danger to his way of life was illustrated in that bit of news.

John Q. did not know what he had read in his newspaper that day. He saw no connection between that story about the Strategic Air Command on page one, and the little news item about a factory down in Louisiana on an inside page of the paper. John Q. American does not know what it takes in today's world to make it possible for him to continue to do the things that Cubans, Indians, Chinese, and Africans are not doing as well as he does.

There is a connection, a very important one, between that kind of newspaper item and a world map. Two of the simplest sources of history are newspaper clippings and maps. Over a period of time I have kept a record on a world map, marking with red thumbtacks the places where communists have been particularly active in the revolutions of non-communist peoples. Another important source of information is the *Minerals Yearbook,* a publication of the United States Department of the Interior. It lists all of the minerals and metals that we use to keep us prosperous in peace and strong in war. About seventy of the minerals listed in this book are particularly important to us because either we do not have them at all, or we do not have enough of them. We have to import these things into the United States.

On another world map I have marked with black thumbtacks the places from which we import these minerals. Those clusters of red and black thumbtacks show one of the most arresting facts about the kind of world in which you and I, and revolutionaries like Juan, José, and Pedro live. The red and black thumbtacks cluster, interestingly enough, in the same

CUBAN REVOLUTION: THE BATTLE OF AMERICA   27

places. In other words, communist interest and communist activity is greatest in areas where the non-communist countries of the world obtain critically important minerals and metals.

With this map and what it shows in mind, we can return to that news item which John Q. American read quickly and forgot promptly. That forty-five-million-dollar plant gathering dust in Port Nickel was a nickel-cobalt refinery that was supposed to make that town the nickel-cobalt capital of the United States. But when the refinery was finished it produced nothing. Why? Because one of the things that Juan, José, and Pedro fought for in Cuba was to put an end to the draining of Cuba's mineral wealth to foreign countries.

Cuba has what may turn out to be the world's most important reserves of nickel-cobalt ore, a special kind of ore. That refinery in Louisiana was specially built to work those ores and no others, because since 1945 we have imported as much as 90 per cent of all the nickel we have used in this country and as much as 85 per cent of the cobalt we have needed. We have to import them. These are the facts underlying that article John Q. read on page one of his newspaper about the Strategic Air Command's round-the-clock program. The engines in those SAC planes are made of metal using nickel and cobalt to resist heat. Without this alloy there would be far fewer SAC planes—which are still our main defense against aggression. Without these metals there would be far fewer rocket engines to power intercontinental ballistic missiles and put satellites into space. There would be far less security for Americans against the danger of military aggression. On my own map I have now marked Cuba off as a source of nickel and cobalt ore for this country. That source was cut off in Chapter One of the Battle of America.

The point in describing this experiment in putting together the elements of history is to make clear the fact (which the world's communist leaders know, but which too many of us do not know) that today whoever controls the world's mineral resources can control the world. Americans must learn that in today's world not one of the so-called western powers, including the United States, has all of the minerals it needs in its own territory. The demands for an investigation of this nation's stockpiling program that began with President Kennedy's announcement in February, 1962, of unnecessary overstocking of several raw materials in no way detracts from this fact. The stockpiles themselves are proof of our dependence on other countries for a variety of materials. We stockpile the things we do not have at all, or do not have in the right quantity or quality. By cutting off or by simply interfering with the easy movement of supplies of raw materials from places like Indochina or Cuba, the economies of the western powers can be weakened. Their economies can be wrecked; and this is one of the most important long-range goals of the Soviet Union and communist China, particularly in Latin America.

The communist powers do not presently need military bases in Cuba or any place outside their own borders to secure these long-range goals. In Latin America, as a starting point, Cuba is important to Russia and Red China most of all as an example to the rest of Latin America. It can show what a people's revolution with communist help can do to realize the things for which Juan, and José, and Pedro, fought.

Cuba is a communist outpost in the Americas. The Castro revolution appealed to Cubans and made them fight so hard because they recognized that Castro represented a revolution which would give them political power. Whether or not it has actually done so, it contains the promise of the good life they have never known. This has just as strong an appeal to the Ecuadorian Indian, or the Peruvian, or the Brazilian Negro. Taken together, Indians and Negroes make up most of the population in Latin America, most of the 90 per cent of Latin America on the poor side of the gulf that Pope John spoke to Cubans about.

On a trip to the U.S.S.R. in 1960, while Castro was consolidating his revolution, I spoke to a half dozen young people from different parts of Latin America who were studying at the University of Moscow. First and most important, their tuition was free; their transportation was paid for. All of these students were from small towns and villages in their respective countries. When they finished their studies they intended to return to those towns and villages. I asked students how they felt about this opportunity to study and learn.

"Very grateful," they told me.

What kind of program put them in that university? It was a special program started by communist China in 1958, and followed by the U.S.S.R. in 1959, to educate and train young Ecuadorians, Bolivians, Peruvians, and other Latins in the ideas and ways of Marxian communism, and in a variety of specially selected subjects. Those young people, after being trained in Moscow, will return to their villages and wait for the day to do the things that have to be done to stabilize any communist revolution. If Castro's revolution prospers, then with communist help the next nineteen chapters of the Battle of America are already largely written. The Latin American students trained in Russia and China will have their chance to step into power in their own countries. There is not much doubt about this. It will happen for very much the same reason that Cuban communists moved into power in Cuba. Fidel Castro could fight a revolution without people trained in economics, or finance, or transportation, or communications, and without experts to run business and industry, and agriculture, but Castro could not stabilize his revolution without such people.

When I asked those young Latin Americans in Moscow what courses they were taking, they told me they were studying economics, finance, transportation, and communications.

Why? Because it is an important characteristic of all revolutions that they leave political, social, and economic vacuums. People who run revolutions obviously do not trust the people that they overthrow. The revolutionaries use effective methods such as the firing squad to make sure that the old guard will not endanger the revolution.

And so the trained technicians and leaders of the old way disappear during revolutions. But the vacuums created by revolutions must be filled. Who was there in Cuba whom Castro and his revolutionaries could trust? No one from the upper or the middle classes, or even from the working class movement, was acceptable. Those groups, they believed, had sided with the Batista government. Who was there in Cuba, among the peasants, particularly from small towns and villages, who could step in after Castro came to power? Where were the noncommunist educated and trained people from the small towns and villages? In other words, what counterforce had we of the West prepared in Cuba? None. The communists moved in by default.

What force are we preparing now while the Soviet Union and communist China are training those young South Americans in special schools? What force did we prepare against the day of revolution that was written for years over the face of Cuba for all the world to see, as it was written all over Asia and Africa, and as it is written all over South America today? The training programs for South American students in Moscow and in Peking are obviously communism's investment in the future, a future that Stalin charted, the same future which Khrushchev has promised the whole world.

What investment did we Americans of the North make in Cuba, in the people? What investments—other than military preparedness—are we thinking of making in Latin America, in Asia and Africa, to insure that the future will not belong to the communists?

A few months before the abortive invasion at the Bay of

Pigs, I talked to Cubans in Miami about the counterrevolution. At one meeting in that city's Flagler Park, a group of Cuban exiles who called themselves the Alliance for Liberation showed *their* burning ambition to see Cuba free—but this time free from Castro. There were many Cuban groups. Most of them were disunited. Most of them were disorganized. But they were all intensely committed to overthrowing Castro.

One group was led by Dr. Antonio Verona, formerly a speaker in Cuba's Senate and later a prime minister. Then he became an exile and a counterrevolutionary, leader of a group called the Autentico Party. Then there was Dr. Eusta Callerio who headed Cuba's Development Bank in the first days after the revolution, where he saw receipts for money sent to agents working for Castro, and to the communists in other Latin countries. Dr. Callerio escaped from Cuba and joined the Democratic Revolutionary Front with Dr. Orelo Sanches Orango, once minister of Cuban education, and strongly anti-Batista.

Or consider Captain Manuel Artime, who left medical school to join Castro and his revolution, only to learn later about Castro's plans to move Cuba into the communist world. He headed a group called the Counterrevolutionary Movement of Revolutionary Recovery. Dr. José Roscoe went to college with Castro. He became the moving force behind the Christian Democratic Movement. Pedro Luis Díaz Lanz, the former head of Castro's Air Force, was the first Cuban official to defect. He came to the United States by small boat and warned a United States Senate investigating committee that the communists were taking control in Cuba. He headed an anti-Castro group called The Cuban Constitutional Crusade.

To back up the hopes of these counterrevolutionary groups, I saw secondhand weapons of all kinds being collected. They were loaded into small boats for increasingly dangerous trips to Cuba; taking in supplies and bringing out refugees and fugitives from Castro's police. Many exiles went back to Cuba to fight even before the April invasion. Many of them died; many went to prison.

Then came the invasion at the Bay of Pigs, and through an unfortunate chain of mismanagement and misinformation, extending from military details to arrangements between the revolutionary groups, the invasion failed. But the failure taught two lessons which must not be lost to Americans:

First, the failure in the Bay of Pigs showed that there was no reasonable alternative to Fidel Castro's government in the spring of 1961. The disorganized counterrevolutionaries were untrained, undisciplined, and unsuited to the job of carrying out an invasion. Even had they succeeded momentarily, they could not have succeeded finally without gigantic doses of American aid, and a lot of luck. They could not have convinced the campesinos that they had not brought American colonialism back to Cuba with them.

Second, the failure showed how completely naive the American government had remained after years of observing postwar revolutionary activity by the communist powers of the world. As a nation we still knew nothing about the true state of affairs in Cuba, and apparently our government knew little more than the governed. There were no cadres of American-trained Cubans who might step into the breach. There had never been an American program to train Latins, or any other foreigners, for this purpose.

Even before the invasion, I wondered how those highly emotional, disorganized revolutionary forces, with no clear-cut program to meet the problems of Cuba, could succeed by turning Cuba into a battleground again.

Was that to be our investment to keep the Battle of America from going communism's way in the other nineteen countries south of the border?

It was. The question is, was that an effective answer?

It was not!

And would the answer be more effective anywhere else in the world? How would arming other counterrevolutionaries solve the problem of land reform? How does transporting troops solve the problem of economic reform? How do planes and bombs bring about industrial development? How does this solve the problem of race prejudice? These are the things that foment revolutions today. What is America's answer? Another day like that in the Bay of Pigs?

Shortly before the invasion I asked Neil MacCauley, the old Castro soldier, what he thought America ought to do; how he thought the situation in Cuba could be resolved; if he believed there was a chance for an invasion to succeed; if he thought the United States should intervene?

Neil MacCauley offered no solution. Why? Because it was too late for one kind of solution, and too soon for another.

MacCauley could see, as most Americans could not, that the exiles, even with support from inside Cuba, had very little chance of success. He knew that the situation got worse as time went by, that with each day the chances of overthrowing Castro diminished. The Russians were sending in arms and equipment, the planes, the tanks, everything Castro needed to put down a popular rebellion, and MacCauley believed the Russians themselves would put it down for Castro if it came to that. "Once the communists get hold of a country they don't let go," MacCauley said.

The subsequent events proved how accurate a prophet Neil MacCauley was. He knew Castro and Cuba as few Americans did.

This story of Cuba should convince all Americans who read it that we live today in the world of Juan, and José, and Pedro, and that we Americans *do not know that world.* From Indonesia around the world to Cuba it is a world of exploding populations desperately in need of reform: land reform, economic reform, agricultural reform, industrial reform; a world sensitive to the point of explosion about the idea held by too many white-skinned people that they are somehow better than dark-skinned people.

These are the important facts of revolutions. The problems existed in human affairs long before the first Bolshevik was out of diapers. Let us not forget that fact. And these same problems would dominate human affairs if every communist on earth were very conveniently to die this minute. Communists didn't create today's revolutions, but they have fed on them for the past forty-five years. Russia's revolution in 1917 was not a communist revolution, but it became one. Nothing did more to keep the communists in power in Russia than the guns and men Russian counterrevolutionary groups received from the United States and other countries. More than three years of bullets and counterrevolution failed to destroy communism in Russia. The bullet hasn't been made that can shoot our way out of the problems that exist in the world of men like Juan, José, and Pedro. We tried the easy answer to problems that have no easy answer.

Cuba is not Russia. With our weapons today, that island could be not only overrun; it could be wiped out in minutes. But Cuba *is* like Russia in the sense that bullets and counterrevolution are no better solutions today for the problems of land reform, or economic reform, or exploding population than they were after the Bolshevik Revolution.

Look hard at recent history as it actually happened. After spending some ninety billion dollars since World War II, despite all our military gifts and all our defensive alliances, all our technical assistance and economic aid, the communists have continued to feed heavily on the stuff that makes revolutions. The communists have taken over other people's revolutions, including the one in Cuba, in our own Western Hemisphere. The two main reasons for this that must be recognized are, first, that the dollar hasn't been printed yet that can buy our way out of the kind of world Juan, Pedro, and José live in.

Second, bullets and counterrevolution are still the easy answers for problems that have no easy answers.

There *are* no easy answers for dealing with the stuff revolutions are made of. There are no easy answers to communism: only hard work. Hard work by each individual thinking and voting American who must learn to understand that the key to the survival of our way of life today lies in dealing with the world of Juan, Pedro, and José. Not just to understand that world, but to work in it, away from the tourist alleys; to defend America not just in the Battle of America which Mr. Castro intends to wage in Latin America, but in the battle which communists intend for the whole world.

This hard work means facing head-on the problems of exploding populations, land reform, and economic reform, and to do this by other means than blank checks passed around by blank minds. Until we do this, it will not be communism that wins the world. It will be democracy that loses it.

CHAPTER 2

The Ugly American—I

IN 1958, TWO INTELLIGENT AMERICANS wrote a novel about Americans overseas. The book was praised and damned throughout this country. It was called *The Ugly American* and dealt with Americans overseas, particularly with those who administered the assistance programs our government has established around the world as one of our principal defenses against communism since the end of World War II. The book presented a disappointing picture of American bumbling in international affairs. The one admirable and intelligent American in the book was the physically ugly American, a simple, honest man who approached the people of the book's mythical, composite land with sympathy, understanding, and a desire to learn. The other Americans in the book tried to behave themselves when abroad exactly as they might have lived at home. They adopted almost all the outer trappings of colonialism, and they seemed to pick up most of the attitudes of the colonialists. These were the truly ugly Americans.

Those Americans did not understand, and it sometimes seems that they will never understand, why the peoples of the world are not grateful to the United States for all this country has done to save the world from communism.

Americans in uniform fought in places like Burma, and China, and throughout the Pacific region to defend and protect what President Roosevelt in 1941 described as the Four Freedoms: freedom of speech, freedom of worship, freedom from want, and freedom from fear. Since the end of World War II Americans, both in and out of uniform, have remained in Southeast Asia still defending those freedoms. Nevertheless headlines from places like Laos and South Viet-Nam suggest that many Southeast Asians do not want those freedoms.

Why not?

The simplest answer is that the Four Freedoms so dear to most of us have no meaning in the societies of most of the world. What we said we were defending for the native peoples of Southeast Asia during World War II was meaningless to almost all of those people. What we have told Southeast Asians we were defending for them since World War II has remained meaningless.

The Ugly American, as we will be concerned about him here, is not the good American. The truly ugly American is the one who does not know, or refuses to accept, the facts of his time.

When the Pacific War began in 1941, practically all Asians knew that the age of colonialism had ended. The Japanese, a colored race, won the first victories. The Japanese told Asians —and proved it—that Asia could be free from western domination.

There was something very important involved in the Burma phase of World War II, something that the American GI on the Ledo Road, or with Merrill's Marauders, did not know. Had he known about it, the American soldier would not have considered it quite so peculiar that many Southeast Asians preferred to fight with the Japanese against us; or against both the Japanese and us. If Americans had then realized the depth of that feeling, it would have been far less shocking to us today to learn that there are Southeast Asians who now prefer to side with the communists against us.

With the attack on Pearl Harbor, the capture of the Philippines, and the fall of Malaya, the people of the five states of Indo-China and the people of Indonesia had gone far beyond the point where they were interested in talk about freedom. Whatever Southeast Asians may have thought of Japanese promises, they needed answers to some very important questions.

What were those questions? First, what kind of political system would be best for people who knew nothing about politics? Second, what political system would give them the type of economy best suited to meet the needs of newly independent states? Third, what social changes must be made to create the freedom to work for them?

We gave them no answers to these questions.

During World War II the Japanese gave some very specific answers. Since World War II the communists have given some very specific answers. We offered Asians the Four Freedoms during World War II. We have given them roads, dams, public health, and foreign aid programs since the war—but no answers to the questions about the best political system for them.

In less than two hundred years of American history, something has happened to Americans that makes it hard for us to define and defend democracy as it must be defined and defended in our time. What happened is the story of the truly ugly American, a story which deals first of all with the Americans at home who have made it impossible for Americans outside the nation to answer the big questions of our time.

As Americans, we have been quick to recognize bravery and sacrifice. Abraham Lincoln once described these as the last full measure of an American's devotion to his country. Our men in uniform, we say on Memorial Day and Veterans' Day, have been worthy of their country. Yet not much is said about an equally important kind of bravery and sacrifice: the sacrifice that measures the devotion of men who, in time of peace and wearing no uniforms, have made this nation worthy of the men who died for it. It is as important that we be worthy of such men who died for us as it is that they be worthy of their country.

No day has been set aside to honor the bravery and sacrifice of Albert Patterson, who was murdered in Phenix City, Alabama. Patterson tried to bring the law back to his home town, then one of the worst crime centers in the nation. Phenix City was overrun with B-girls, prostitutes, poker houses, drug pushers, abortion mills, and an adoption racket. Phenix City was not worthy of the men who died in our wars to keep this country a nation under law. There was no law in Phenix City, nor was there much courage. Public opinion did not support Patterson when he tried to clean up his town. He did so, nevertheless, despite bombings, beatings, threats, and the resentment of people who could not understand why Patterson would not leave well enough alone. For a time, the people of Phenix City enjoyed somewhat more dignified lives because one man had the courage to fight for the principles in which he believed. No honored man in uniform died more bravely or sacrificed more in war than Albert Patterson did in peace.

In Florida in 1959, ninety men gathered in a room in the State House, to hold a special meeting of the State Legislature. The meeting had been called by the Governor to pass laws to evade the U. S. Supreme Court ruling that the color of the human skin should in no way affect a child's right to the best possible education. Eighty-nine of the men in Florida's

House of Representatives voted to pass those laws. One did not. His name was John Orr, Jr. Orr said he would not be pushed by public opinion. He rose in that hall to say that the democratic principles for which so many of our fighting men had died—black-skinned men as well as white-skinned men—were too important to be thrown aside by the Florida Legislature that day. Segregation, second-class citizenship, had no place in Florida or in the nation, he said, speaking to a shocked and silent House.

That day marked the beginning of John Orr's trial by fire. His enemies tried to oust him from office and from his party. He was given the silent treatment and threatened. Bravery of that kind in peace was as great as any fighting man's bravery was in war. By what such men do our democratic ideas become worthier of the men who die for them?

The Pattersons, the Tom Paines, and the Patrick Henrys of our history would not bow to ignorance, or bigotry, or apathy. They hated the attitudes and actions that make Americans ugly at home and in the surrounding world. Those brave individuals made this a nation governed by laws that protect freedom. They gave Americans a human dignity worth fighting and dying for.

It has been estimated that the human race has passed thirty-five million laws trying, as one writer put it, to enforce ten simple commandments. This is more than just a wisecrack. It is not important whether the figure of thirty-five million laws is anywhere near the number of rules and regulations which have been developed throughout history. What is important is that laws have not yet made America the kind of nation, or made the world the kind of place, where the Ten Commandments can work.

There are a number of reasons for this sad state of affairs. Not the least of them is the fact that ideas about the right way to do things simply are not the same in one place as they are in another. For example, in some parts of the world it has either been proper at one time, or is considered to be proper now, for a man to marry his mother, his sister, his aunt, his daughter, or his first cousin. Our ideas about this matter differ, and our laws show the difference. In the time of the ancient Hebrews, King Solomon once said that it was proper for a man to take as many wives as he could support. Several of the American Indian tribes claimed that a man had the right to as many wives as were necessary to support him—obviously a much better arrangement. In Tibet, to this day, it is not considered improper for a woman to marry several husbands. In several other lands, when a girl marries she takes not just her husband but all his brothers, too.

We do not accept these rules of conduct, and our laws show that we do not.

It is possible to draw up a list of differences among peoples' ideas about what is right or wrong in human affairs. That list would fill several books. The laws by which people live express their ideas. Laws express the customs people have worked out while evolving a way of life. People make their customs and practices legal and binding among themselves. Laws come after the ideas, customs, and practices have been worked out, not before. That is why the Ten Commandments cannot be ordered into existence by law. Any commandment, however derived, must first be accepted as the basis for the way people think and act. Then laws based on the Commandments might be workable.

This has not been possible in most of the world. It is not possible now to pass such laws because most of the people of the world do not accept the Ten Commandments as valid rules of conduct. This does not apply only to Tibetans, Fijians, Eskimos, and Indians. It applies also to a very large number of Americans in these fifty United States who, in their dealings with each other in politics, business, religion, and education, behave as though they had never heard of the Ten Commandments.

In any event, these commandments today cannot be enforced. They can only be accepted and respected, as the
Pattersons, the Tom Paines, and the Patrick Henrys respected
them, and fought for them, to make the lives of the rest of
us richer and better.

A day should be set aside for such men and women not
so much because of what they did, but because their actions
made clear the basis of our way of life, and what we have
to offer the world.

We offer the opportunity for brave men to think, to question, to investigate, and to act on their conclusions. This opportunity alone makes what we represent to the rest of the world
worth dying for: Freedom of the mind for those brave enough
to use it.

It takes a brave man to use such freedom, because that freedom is not respected by many of today's Americans, any more
than it was respected by many of yesterday's Americans. It
takes bravery to be the kind of unconforming individual who
thinks for himself about more important things than filter
cigarettes. It takes brave men to wipe out crime and corruption in an American city. It takes a strong man to stand
for Christ's Second Commandment—to love thy neighbor as
thyself—in Florida's State Legislature.

During our early history such men practicing such courage
strengthened our determination to fight a revolution to be
free. But how much bravery does it take for a man to use
freedom to think, question, investigate, and act in ordinary
life today?

The degree of courage needed is made frighteningly clear
by such things as a personnel pamphlet distributed a few
years ago by one of the nation's largest oil companies. The
oil company advised college students how to behave while in
college if they expected to be employed by that company after
graduation. Here is a paragraph from the pamphlet:

"Personal views can cause a lot of trouble. All 'isms' are out.

Business being what it is, it looks with disfavor on the radical —or even the moderate pink."

Just what that oil company considered to be a "radical" or a "pink" was not spelled out anywhere in the pamphlet. Who are the radicals? They could be the Pattersons, the Adamses, and the Patrick Henrys of our history—all of them were men with strong personal views. They could be the signers of the Declaration of Independence. Perhaps Thomas Jefferson and Robert E. Lee could not qualify for employment by that company. They had strong personal views. So did Plato, Pericles, Voltaire and Einstein. So did Jesus Christ. These men—the troublemakers who made history—would have been poor job prospects for that American oil company.

In attacking "isms," the pamphlet helps explain why so few of America's young people know anything about Americanism, let alone the other isms. But they will have to deal with these isms when today's older Americans who do not respect freedom of the mind are dead and gone.

It takes a brave man to use freedom in the face of this kind of anti-Americanism.

About the time that I received the oil company's pamphlet, I learned of a Congressional investigation being conducted in Washington. This investigation was concerned with work being done by institutes and foundations. The investigators were worried that the foundations and others might support the work of people who could be the "troublemakers" of our time. The investigators paid no attention to the fact that "troublemakers" like Henry Ford, Thomas Edison, and Albert Einstein were among the dangerous men whose thinking changed America. The report of that Congressional committee warned our Ford and Rockefeller Foundations—and through them our university faculties and other research centers—*not* to change things.

"The trustees of foundations," said the report, "should be very careful about supporting the work of men whose ideas, concepts, and opinions seem against what the public currently wishes, approves, and likes."

Obviously neither that oil company nor that Congressional investigating committee would have supported Christianity and the Ten Commandments two thousand years ago. There is some evidence that the public of Christ's day did not wish to be disturbed by Christ's teachings. That public did not approve or like what Christ had to say.

Using this same logic, that oil company itself would not exist today if the public's wishes had been followed in the matter of the automobile in the early years of this century. Nor would we have the airplane, the steamboat, the telephone, the radio, and hundreds of the things thinking men gave us to make us what we are today. Progress has never been made or "liked" by the public. No committee ever invented anything: only individual human beings, of all races, invented things and brought new ideas to mankind, from the earliest civilization down to our own. But let us not forget that every man with a new idea was a pariah until the idea was proved right. The idea men, the troublemakers were successful not because they honored the public's wishes, but through opposing them, the way the Albert Pattersons and John Orrs did in our time.

Such men acted in defense of principle: the principle of human dignity. It is possible to do this only in a nation ruled by law, under which all men, regardless of race, creed, or color, have the right to stand before their God and their fellow men as dignified human beings. There is no more powerful principle in the world today, whether it is in Christian teaching, or Moslem, or Buddhist, or Jewish, or any other.

Race, creed, and color. Those three words are easily the most misunderstood, misused, and abused words in the English language. Certainly, the idea of "creed" was misunderstood by the men who made possible that Congressional report, and the oil company's pamphlet, in the middle of Twentieth Century America.

For, like most people, the men of the committee and the oil company, who rattle off the words "race, creed, and color," showed that they do not really know the meaning of the words. Creed, for example, has a simple meaning: it is a confession of a man's faith; his religious faith, and his political, social, economic, and philosophical beliefs. This applies to Americans as people of a nation. We have an American creed. It consists of the things we have believed as we made ourselves one of history's great nations. The American creed encompasses one of the widest ranges of faiths and beliefs in history. We have had freedom, under law, to think freely, to question freely, to investigate freely, and to act freely.

But today the creed that made us great is under fire by men in government, men in business, men in labor, and even men in the church. They would like to see our range of freedom narrowed down to a set of faiths and beliefs approved by them. They want a safer, more manageable set of faiths and beliefs, something less risky, less challenging, than the old.

This attitude is not just un-American; it is *anti*-American. The American creed was based originally on the idea of risk. What riskier situation has there been in all history than the one that began less than two hundred years ago when people living in thirteen American colonies decided that they would govern themselves? Every proper government on earth then was shocked. American independence was dangerous to kings, and princes, and petty tyrants. Across the world, almost all governments wished the Founding Fathers ill, and hoped the new nation would fail. Instead, that risky venture turned into the way of life we now enjoy, offering more freedom to think, act, and live than has ever been known before. All through our history we have accepted the risk of failure. How could people live and work together with such widely divergent faiths and beliefs? It seemed impossible to the rest of the world that the American melting pot could ever produce one nation of people.

Well, the story of our success should be told and retold, so that young people today will understand Americanism, and the American creed. The separate backgrounds, the diverse faiths and beliefs have turned out to be our greatest strength—not at all a weakness. The different ways that Poles, Germans, Irish, Italian, Russians, and Chinese thought and acted were forged into a way of life that has made us the wealthiest and most powerful people on earth. This great success was not realized under conditions in which men were forced to conform to an approved pattern. America was made great by men and women who risked their lives, their money, and their labor. Today the children of those brave ones are being pressured by small, frightened minds to become security conscious instead of risk conscious.

It is not possible to have your cake and eat it too, as any child knows. The security such people want, and the freedoms of our history—based on risk—are not compatible. You cannot achieve security by passing laws or by suppressing ideas. This routine is age old; it has never worked. Security cannot be forced by business pressure, it cannot be legislated by government. Like the Ten Commandments, security cannot be "lawed" into existence, and for the same reason. You cannot legislate loyalty. You cannot legislate honesty. You cannot legislate human dignity. Like the Ten Commandments these are articles of faith, they must be accepted and practiced by each person.

America's businessmen once believed that there was nothing like competition between people in a free market to produce the best possible product. The stiffer the competition, they said, the better the product. This nation once believed, too, that there was nothing like competition between ideas in a free country to produce the best thinkers. In economics, and in politics, those old principles have weakened, and that Congressional committee report, and the oil company's advice (and they are only a few of many), show how far the United States has traveled since the days of the Founding Fathers.

In our time, there is as great a need as there ever was for brave men who know that it takes more than lip service to our traditions in Memorial Day and Veterans' Day speeches to make us what the last line of our national anthem says we are: *"the land of the free and the home of the brave."* It takes brave men to fight those who fear differences in faith and belief, here at home and in the rest of the world. It takes brave men who know that if we succeed in wiping out those differences; if we succeed in keeping Americans from thinking about "isms" and from having "strong personal views"; if we succeed in wiping out all radicals, all odd-balls, all the troublemakers who make history, then we will destroy our greatest strength. And we *will* do exactly that if we fail to recognize that it was the odd-balls, the troublemakers, and the radicals (whatever that word means) who made it possible for us to enjoy a greater degree of human dignity than most of the world has known. As long as we have the Patterson, Orrs, Paines, and Patrick Henrys with us, this will be the land of the free because it is the home of the brave.

CHAPTER 3

The Ugly American—II

IN 1945, AS THE JAPANESE soldiers in Indo-China prepared
to surrender their arms in the northern capital city of Hanoi,
a small, thin, tubercular man with a stringy beard moved
quietly into the city. His ragged guerrillas captured the white
building near the Metropole Hotel that housed the French
general government. They strung barbed wire around the
government building to keep out the French and the Chinese
who would soon occupy the area. Then they proclaimed a
rebel government of Viet-Nam. The man's name was Ho Chi
Minh. He was a trained communist who had served time in
the Comintern revolutionary headquarters in Moscow as
well as in a British prison in Hongkong.

Nine years later, in June, 1954, at the Ben Hai River, Indo-
China was cut in half by this same man. Refugees, seven hundred thousand of them, began pouring across the river before
it became a boundary between the communist state of North
Viet-Nam and a non-communist South Viet-Nam.

48

What happened in those nine years? And what did it have to do with Americans?

For one thing, Americans spent more than two billion dollars to prevent just what did happen, the partition of Indo-China into communist and non-communist territories. We spent that money, and we lost.

World War II may have ended for Americans on V-J Day in 1945, but for the French and the peoples of Indo-China it did not end until July 21, 1954, almost ten years later. And before it was over, France had poured over five billion dollars into the Indo-Chinese fighting. Since it ended, we have given the non-communist South Viet-Namese government as much as a quarter of a billion dollars a year to stay in business as insurance against a repeat performance.

We are fighting, interestingly enough, to keep the communists from doing in the Sixties what Imperial Japan had done in Southeast Asia during the Forties. Japan moved into Indo-China in 1940, intending to use it as a jumping-off place for the conquest of all Southern Asia—to move through India to the oil-soaked Middle East. Until V-J Day, Japan did dominate all Southeast Asia from Indo-China. American military men and our policy planners have worked since then to prevent a repetition of this by the communists.

The splitting of Indo-China in 1954 gave the communists their springboard in that part of the world. Headlines from Laos, Thailand, and South Viet-Nam show that the communists have been using their advantage well in one of the most important, strategic, and potentially richest areas on earth.

Headlines from South Viet-Nam, though, show more. In 1954 those seven hundred thousand refugees moved from Northern Indo-China to live in what was described as "freedom" in the South. Our government made the Viet-Namese understand that we would support and protect freedom for all who would come south. Headlines from South Viet-Nam made it very clear that many Viet-Namese did not see much more freedom in South Viet-Nam than they had seen in the communist North.

Dissident non-communist Viet-Namese staged an unsuccessful revolt against the South Viet-Nam government, the government we have been supporting with a quarter billion dollars a year. America still is not popular in Viet-Nam—even after spending billions of dollars and years of effort to do a very necessary job there.

The news from Southeast Asia about American unpopularity should have a familiar ring by this time. Despite more billions of dollars and more years of effort to do the same necessary job, the same story has been coming out of places like Korea and Japan in the Far East, and Turkey in the Near East.

As with the South Viet-Namese, South Koreans did not see much more freedom under Syngman Rhee in the South than in the communist North, although we supported the Rhee government for fifteen years.

Quite a few Asian countries, with unhappy memories about the Imperial Japanese occupation during World War II, still cannot understand how we could support men like the former Prime Minister of Japan, Nobusuke Kishi. Our own judges once called him a war criminal.

Similarly, no small number of Americans were somewhat surprised, after reading so many nice things in our press about Adnan Menderes in Turkey, to learn that a large number of Turks who were not communists saw him as anything but a defender of freedom and democracy. The Turks threw Menderes out of office and into jail, despite the fact that he was our man in Istanbul, and finally they hung him as a criminal.

Now, what goes on here? Why do we have this record of backing "wrong horses" in so many places that are vital to the United States? Can it be that the important job we are trying to do is not important to the people in those places? Can it be that we do not see things in those places as the people there see them? It can be, and it is the truth. There are reasons for the feeling these people have against Americans.

Early in 1943 in Bengal, then part of eastern India, the British Indian government brought thousands of workmen to build military roads, airfields, and barracks for the American and British troops who were there to defend India, and who were later to recapture Southeast Asia from the Japanese. The American GIs who would use these military installations and facilities were in India to do the same important job in war that we have been trying to do ever since, in Southeast Asia, in the Far East, and in the Near East. Americans were there to defend the Four Freedoms against totalitarian aggression.

For three million Bengalese, however, making the world safe for the Four Freedoms, or for anything else, became irrelevant a few months after they started work for the Allies. By that time, the three million Bengalese were dead—unlisted casualties of World War II. They died from starvation during the terrible famine of 1943.

That same summer, American Superfortresses bombed Japan for the first time. Americans died on lonely Pacific islands. General MacArthur waded ashore in the Philippines. The U. S. Navy fought the second battle of the Philippine Sea. All the exciting news of victories crowded out the news that all around the new installations built for our soldiers in Bengal was famine.

Even if there had been room in the papers for such news at the time, what was so special about starving Bengalese? People "out there" were always starving. If it was not the starving Bengalese, then it was the starving Armenians, or the starving Chinese. If those A-rabs, or Chinks, or Wogs or Gooks knew any better, they would use some get-up-and-go. They would work harder to grow enough food so they would not have to starve. "Whaddya expect from those ignorant, backward savages, anyway?" That was a common American refrain.

Well, for one thing you might expect that those people would not be killed by their friends. I think it is safe to say that almost all Americans, at home or in India, in 1943 considered themselves friends of the Bengalese. Those who knew about that famine in 1943, particularly American troops on the spot, were shocked to see close-up for the first time what hunger could do. They would have been even more shocked had they known the main reason for the famine that surrounded them.

They were the reason.

To this day, few of the men who were in those military bases in Bengal know this fact. Although they could see famine around them, they could not see the kind of world in which the Bengalese lived. It was a world which friendly Americans disrupted, costing British India more people in one year than the cost in human life of *all* of America's wars since the Revolution.

If they had lived in 1776, those soldiers would have known that same kind of world. The American of the Eighteenth Century was very close to that world. Americans then, like the Bengalese in 1943, were mostly farmers. They worked with simple hand tools, and in most cases managed to grow just enough food to last the farmer and his family through one year. Usually there was not much left over to sell for profit.

This kind of farming, common to Eighteenth Century America and Twentieth Century India, is called subsistence farming. In many parts of early America, if you took a man away from his farm for one growing season, or if his crop failed just once, he and his family could starve to death. Many Americans did starve. And this is what happened in Bengal. Many such subsistence farmers were taken away from their farms in 1943 to work on those military construction projects. Thousands of other workers were brought in. They were paid in money, but money does not grow food—men do. So the men building military roads and airfields for us did not grow any food; and soon there were only limited quantities available, not enough to go around.

To get what food there was, the workers offered to pay so much that the local farmers sold their own supply—because most subsistence farmers in Asia were and are up to their ears in debt. The farmers sold their food to the construction workers, hoping to turn around and buy some from other farmers with their profits. But by that time there was no food to buy. American and British troops got their roads, airfields, and barracks in 1943, but at a cost that cannot be measured in money. What is the money value of three million Bengalese lives?

This Bengal famine is now a forgotten incident for most of us, but it is not just the unfortunate history of some faraway place. It is the same kind of event that is taking place right now in very nearby places, as near as Venezuela, Cuba, and Argentina, on our side of the world. We needed airfields and barracks in Bengal in 1943. We need oil, iron, nickel, and cobalt from South America now. There is a price for this. So far, deaths in Bengal, riots in Caracas, and revolution in Cuba are part of that price because of the way we have gone about getting what we need.

The ugly American cannot see this. He cannot understand what happened in Bengal, or in South Korea, or in South Viet-Nam in 1960. The ugly American is simply an uninformed and ignorant American. He is uninformed about the kind of world in which he lives. He is ignorant about how and why the things he sees and considers important in the world are not the things Turks, Koreans, Viet-Namese and most of the rest of the human race consider important.

During World War II, we Americans stated our case, what we as a nation considered important, worth working, fighting, and dying for. We said the Four Freedoms were worth such sacrifice. We were so busy fighting to make the world a safe place, most of us did not hear the joke making the rounds in India at the time of that Bengal famine:

"If you offered an Asian a choice of the Four Freedoms or four sandwiches, he would take the four sandwiches."

Now, this was no measure of the backwardness or the ignorance of Asians; it was a measure of how far we had moved in 165 years—between 1776 and 1941—away from understanding what things were first for men.

Back in 1776 there wasn't any doubt in America about what things were first for men. On June 11, 1776, Thomas Jefferson sat down with Livingston and Franklin and Sherman to draw up a formal statement about what people then living in North America knew was most important in their affairs. They marshaled facts to justify going it alone as an independent state. Thomas Jefferson made his report on July 2 of that year. What he said then would make a lot more sense to the people of the world today than what Americans had to say about Four Freedoms 165 years later, or right now. All men, said Jefferson, have, among other unalienable rights, the right to life, liberty, and the pursuit of happiness.

Who does not know that? Who does not know that those words are the heart of American life—the most important thing in our Declaration of Independence? Everybody knows that.

Well, if everybody does know that, everybody happens to be wrong. The most important thing about the Declaration of Independence is not what it says about man's unalienable rights, but the order in which those rights are listed. We have moved a long way away from understanding the world we live in, a long way from understanding why anybody would prefer four sandwiches to Four Freedoms, a long way from understanding what things come first in human affairs anywhere, because Americans of the Twentieth Century do not understand the significance of Jefferson's order of things in Eighteenth Century America.

What is that order? First came *life*: this means food in the stomach; the first of all things first. If you find this hard to believe, go back to the order that early Christians understood much better than today's Christians do—an order clear in the Lord's Prayer:

"Give us this day our daily bread," the Prayer begins. Only second are the words "Forgive us . . ." Bread, for life, comes first. After that, other things become possible, things like the second listed, after life, in the American Declaration of Independence: liberty. Then, after liberty, comes the pursuit of happiness.

First things come first. The Founding Fathers knew that. Most of the world knows it now but Americans who trooped around the world offering the human race the Four Freedoms did not know it, any more than most of today's Americans administering technical assistance programs around the world really know it now.

The first of the Four Freedoms we talk about is freedom of speech. This is followed by freedoms to assemble and worship; and then, at the end, comes freedom from want and fear. This is an important difference because the American order of freedoms is irrelevant for most of the human race. It is backwards.

Between our Declaration of Independence, for which we fought a revolution, and the declaration of Four Freedoms, for which we fought and worked during the past twenty years, there is a world of difference. We belong to the world of full stomachs as against the world of empty ones. This is the real, the basic, division in the world today, not the one about which full-stomached Russians and full-stomached Americans are belaboring the world. An interest in either communism or democracy is a luxury only the well-fed can afford. For in most of the world, the problem of life is first; and there are other ways to tackle that problem than by turning to either communism or democracy.

A good dose of hunger would be the surest and quickest cure for the disease that afflicts the ugly American. Maybe then he would get to know the kind of world he lives in.

Since World War II Americans have been talking to the underprivileged of the world about the benefits and advantages of freedom and democracy. Our Voice of America broadcasts this message from several parts of the world. Our United States Information Agency (USIA) prints the message from local libraries and information centers all over the world. We have sponsored a variety of programs intended to help the poor in other lands live a healthier, better life.

This is where we have been spending those billions of dollars, and years of effort. In many of the places where we have spent the most and worked the hardest, we have not received our money's worth; around the world they say unkind things about us; they throw over the governments we back.

But, what have we been saying to those people? More important, to whom have we been talking?

Adnan Menderes, in Turkey, knew at least the trappings of freedom and democracy. But what about Turkiye Cumuryeti, the shepherd in Anatolia, who does not? Syngman Rhee in Korea knew about freedom and democracy. Daehan Minkuk, farmer, does not know. Nobusuke Kishi in Japan knew about freedom and democracy, having been one of the leaders of Imperial Japan who fought against it from Pearl Harbor to V-J Day. Dai Hitori, fisherman, does not know.

To whom have we been talking all these years?

Menderes, Rhee, Kishi, Souvanna Phouma of Laos, have all heard the Voice of America on their radios. They could read the booklets and pamphlets of the USIA. They had an understanding of the science and technology involved in the work of our aid programs. But Turkiye Cumuryeti, shepherd,

Daehan Minkuk, farmer, and Dai Hitori, fisherman, have no radios, they cannot read, and they know little or nothing about science and technology. Whom have we been addressing, and what have we been saying? Do we really know?

A few years back, some of our hard-earned billions of dollars were spent to beam messages into Asia from a radio ship which anchored in different places from time to time, and spoke in glowing terms to anyone who could hear about the benefits and advantages of freedom, individualism, and capitalism. For some reason, those broadcasts created more resentment than good will among Asians who tuned in, and so the ship returned home. Our government was not in Asia to make enemies.

What went wrong? Were there communist agents on that ship? No, the ship was full of 100 per cent red-blooded Americans, most of them uninformed and ignorant about the important facts of life in Asia.

Many Asians believe in predestination as part of their religion. They are certain that it is indecent—immoral, in fact—for men to try to change the basic order of life. Life is as it is in the world, because all things were decided long ago. It was Allah's will, or God's will, or as Buddha said, that things be as they are. Man's future was decided long ago, and man had little to say about it. To those people our radio ship said: The future is yours to decide; be rugged individualists; be free. What we said did not make friends for us.

There are not many people in the world today who believe, as we do, that everyone has the right to make his own political, economic, social, or religious decisions. For example, all human beings, wherever they are on this planet, whatever their level of civilization, have three major decisions to make during their lifetime.

One basic decision is the choice of a life's work. By and large, Americans make independent decisions about this, from choosing to be a bus driver to choosing to run for president.

For most of the human race, in South America, as in Africa, as in Asia, there is no such choice. There the youth's way of life is predestined. His economic place is fixed. If his father was a farmer, his father before him was too, and he will be in his time.

A second major choice is the choice of a mate. There are lines all but the most rugged of the free and individualistic Americans will not cross in making this choice, because of racial blocks, or religious or social blocks. But by and large, boy marries girl here as a matter of individual choice. For most of the human race, however, a man cannot marry outside his group or outside his religion. Marriage is out of the hands of boy or girl and in the hands of brokers and parents, to be worked out as an economic or social arrangement.

The final choice is in the matter of religion. By and large, if religious problems become more than a social problem for an American, and deep thought convinces him that he would be happier as a Catholic, or an Episcopalian, or a Congregationalist, or an animist than as whatever he happens to be, he can and does switch religion. This is not the case in most of the rest of the world. A man's religion is not a matter of choice. It was predestined. Religions, and the moral principles by which men live, are the same for them as they were for their parents.

All this is important, very important to Americans today, because few amongst us understand these facts. Before his election, President Kennedy suggested that we organize a Peace Corps of young people from this country who would serve overseas as living, breathing examples of the American Way. After Mr. Kennedy's inauguration the Peace Corps came into being.

There are some indications that the Peace Corps can fail, indications from young Americans overseas. Consider the well-known case of the young college graduate in Nigeria who had been so unwise as to note observations critical of her new

surroundings on the back of a postcard, and then so unfortunate as to drop the postcard, and have it found by someone
who exposed it to the public eye.

Was that finder a communist?

Not necessarily. He may have been an ordinary Nigerian
student, neither communist nor convinced about any political
system. But one thing can be certain: whoever found that postcard was a Nigerian nationalist, an intense youth who had
already made sacrifices, had already broken with an old way
of life in order to find something new. How do I know that?
Because the person who found that postcard could read, and
a Nigerian who could read could not help but be an intense
nationalist in those first days of Nigeria's struggle to enter the
Twentieth Century. Otherwise he would never have made the
effort to learn to read.

There is more that is revealing about the postcard incident
and the young college girl. Her criticism of Nigeria showed
a sense of shock at the primitive nature of Nigerian society.
She was, then, an ugly American, who had been sent to a
foreign land without adequate training, without adequate
background, without even the negative warning that she must
expect life to be lived on an entirely different level.

Actually, after her initial blunder, the young lady from
America behaved with dignity. She did not try to deny the
incident. She did not amplify. She did not cry out or become
angry. She waited; she learned how deep was the feeling she
had aroused among the Nigerian people; and wisely, she left
the country. Her intentions were excellent. She gave further
evidence of sincerity by seeking another job with the Peace
Corps in another land.

Unfortunately, sincerity does not win wars, hot ones or
cold ones. The man you have just mortally insulted does not
forgive you because you did not know he was so sensitive.
The bloodiest Indian uprising of the Nineteenth Century came
after supernationalist Indian Moslems convinced Moslem sol-

diers that they were being polluted by grease from swine—a violation of the Moslem religious code. The fact was that in India, rifle cartridges were packed in grease, and in the past that grease had occasionally been rendered from swine. If British cartridge manufacturers in England offered this insult to the Moslem troops innocently, it made no difference. The damage was done, and hundreds of Englishmen paid for it with their lives. In the Nineteenth Century, and in the Twentieth, innocence has never been an excuse in international relations.

Most troubling about the incident of the young American girl in Nigeria is the fact that American government officials tried to make light of the incident. The claim was made that those who complained in Nigeria were malcontents, with a strong hint that they were communists. Our government also indicated that those who complained in America were also malcontents, with a strong hint that they were not as 100 per cent American as they ought to be.

The worst aspect of the incident was the failure of our government leaders to understand why the incident had happened, and to take the steps necessary to prevent it from happening again.

The necessary steps must lead us to a new point of view toward the people and the country involved. Americans have no inherent right to go to these countries and criticize. When we go with an attitude of comparison with our own country, or of criticism, we cannot possibly do the job at hand.

The United States has no monopoly on uninformed and ignorant people, of the type Captain William Lederer and Eugene Burdick wrote about in *The Ugly American*. All countries suffer from such people, including our competitors for world leadership: the Soviet Russians. There are ugly Russians—just as ugly, just as uninformed, and just as ignorant about things as the ugly American. But that kind of Russian isn't allowed out of the country.

This is a point that bears hard on the Peace Corps. Few more worthwhile ideas have ever been generated in our history. But there is a great danger involved. Until now, except for a few in government service, young, ignorant Americans have gotten around, rather haphazardly, on their own. There has been no deliberate policy to flood the world with what amounts to uninformed Americans.

This not only can but will happen unless we set up adequate training programs for them that will deal with the variety of problems briefly considered in this chapter. Our schools and colleges could do this if you saw the problem, recognized its importance, and wanted them to prepare tomorrow's Americans to meet it.

The decision is in your hands: whether the book *The Ugly American* tells our entire story, or whether that book is to be no more than Chapter One in a story of American success abroad that has yet to be written.

CHAPTER 4

Order of Battle

CHAPTER THREE of the Battle of Asia began late in 1952, when troops of Ho Chi Minh's Viet-Minh government began to march into Laos. Early in 1953, four divisions of Viet-Minh troops crossed the border into Laos. They headed straight across the country, meeting no opposition, and the world waited. The King of Laos, Sisavang Vong, waited in his capital for the communist-led troops to arrive. Suddenly, for no apparent reason, the four Viet-Minh divisions turned around and headed back the way they came, after making one stop, at the town of Sam Neua.

There was talk at the time about the "inscrutable, unpredictable" oriental mind. Why move troops into a country, then out again, without doing anything?

The next year, 1954, the same thing happened. This time they stopped off in the nearby province of Phong Saly. Now here was a puzzler! What were those communist Southeast Asians up to?

62

The events of 1953 and 1954 were repeated in later, minor invasions. Despite the recognition in America that what was happening in Laos was serious, the inscrutable seemed still inscrutable. Events in Laos still seemed unpredictable. It seemed to be a case of "Chaos in Laos," as several of our magazines, newspapers, and newscasters put it.

How can anyone make sense of events in a country that has a railroad station but no railroad? Laos has no year-round roads to connect ten thousand towns which dot a territory the size of the state of Kansas. There are less than five thousand telephones to serve two million people. It has no radio communications.

One way to make some sense of events in Laos would be to do a little arithmetic. In the last six years our government has given more than three hundred million dollars to less than two million Laotians. Statistics show that on a per person basis we have laid out more money in Laos than anywhere else in the world.

How is it then that in the Laotian capital of Vientiane half of all children die before they are ten years old? Outside the capital, where there are almost no medicines and medical care, as many as two-thirds of all children die before they are ten. What is the explanation for the fact that almost everyone in that country is sick, suffering from malnutrition (just plain hunger), malaria, tuberculosis, parasites, or skin infections? Why, after years of financial aid, is Laos one of the poorest nations in the world, with only two factories in the entire country—a tobacco factory and a tin mine?

Why do 95 per cent of these people live as farmers? Why do many of them think the world is flat? Why do they not know they live in a country called Laos?

Is there any connection between this backwardness and those odd "invasions" in places like the jungle town of Sam Neua where that first communist invasion force stopped back in 1953, and nearby Phong Saly, where that second communist invasion force stopped in 1954? Can the miserable conditions in Laos today be connected to the fact that every one of those Laotian soldiers has tied up in his equipment and in his training more than eight thousand United States dollars?

That figure is low. But do some quick arithmetic. The Laotian Army consists of twenty-five thousand men. Nearly 90 per cent of the three hundred million dollars we have given Laos has been spent to carry out the main point of our foreign policy since World War II: to contain communism mainly by military means, even though the facts suggest that communism cannot be contained this way.

Nine years of military power in Indo-China did not contain communism in Indo-China. Chapter Two in the Battle of Asia was written there in 1954. For some not-at-all-inscrutable reasons, military power will not stop the writing of Chapter Three of the Battle of Asia, either. Why not? The answer lies in what happened in Sam Neua and Phong Saly.

Chapter Three in the Battle of Asia illustrates the truth of a statement made long ago by Mao Tse-tung, leader of the Chinese communists.

A long time ago, after he had taken the Chinese communists on the long march from the Yangtze River basin to the northwest frontier area to escape the pursuing forces of Chiang Kai-shek's victorious nationalist armies, Mao Tse-tung sat in a cave in Yenan, a city in northwest China. His revolution, which had followed the Russian pattern, had failed. Now Mao did some hard thinking. He decided that the road of Chinese communism must be redirected. The Russian path had been the wrong path for him. Mao began to write down his thoughts. Before he had finished, Mao had written a series of books and manuals to direct the growth of Chinese communism.

And what was that? It was a new communism, one you have heard little about to date. But one thing is certain: You will hear more of Mao's new brand of communism in the future.

We in the United States know something about the traditional sources and strengths of communist power as it grew in Europe. Communist power there grew from the thinking of two Europeans. Back in 1848, Karl Marx and Friedrich Engels wrote a pamphlet that changed the world. It was *The Communist Manifesto*. Only a handful of Americans have actually read this book, and so only a few Americans understand why it would be possible to contain Russian communism in Europe with foreign aid and military assistance programs, like those we gave the French in Indo-China, and the aid we are still pushing in Laos. But very few Americans understand from that pamphlet why we cannot contain Chinese communism by the same means. The reason is that there are basic differences between the two communist systems.

The heart of the communist revolution of Marx and Engels lay in an industrialized, citified people. The communist revolution Marx hoped for was supposed to result from the fact that people, workers who had only their labor or skills to sell, would rebel against poor pay, frightful working conditions, and inferior social position. They were to be the backbone of Marx's proletarian revolution to set up first a socialist, then a communist society.

Within wide limits, this is the theoretical basis of the Soviet system of socialism. But whatever the official Soviet views about Russian history before communism may be, the Russians did not start from scratch under Lenin to become an industrial power. Industries existed in Russia before the communists came to power. Those industries were badly mangled by World War I and civil war, but they were there. They could be rebuilt.

We in America are an industrial, city-dwelling people. Over 90 per cent of us work in offices, shops, and factories; not on farms. Almost 90 per cent of us live in what can be called urban communities—cities and towns. You do not have to agree with Marx's views of society but you can understand what he is talking about. You can answer the Marxian arguments with American arguments.

But Marx's arguments are not the arguments that Mao Tse-tung and the communist Chinese followed in setting up their communist state. The shape of communism for Marx, Engels, Lenin, and Stalin could not be made to fit communism in China where industrial workers in the cities were so few as to be insignificant. Power in China was not in the hands of the city people. Chinese farmers could and did get along without factory workers. To bring about communist power in China, Mao Tse-tung discarded the European diagram for a communist world and set up a new one which disturbs the U.S.S.R. today only a little less than it bothers those Americans who can see that the actions of a communist power with the farmer as the pillar of the revolution are anything but inscrutable.

In 1949 and 1950, many of us were busily criticizing our State Department for "losing China." Many of us sneered at the communist claim that they were "agrarian reformers." But that claim was not a joke. The Chinese communists did reform agriculture, through collectives and communes, into a kind of political power which is now behind much of the strife in Asia. Those who say the State Department "lost" China do not understand the problems of subsistence farmers, who follow an intensive, and usually single crop, agriculture with the most primitive tools. Those same men and women who shouted the loudest about "losing China" now hold the dangerous idea that military power is the main deterrent to communism.

The Chinese communists built their power on primitive subsistence farmers like those in Laos. For people who still think the world is flat, who do not know the name of the country they live in, who have hardly been touched by the Twentieth Century, the shortcomings or evils of communism or the benefits and advantages of democracy as political or economic systems are just a bit out of their world, beyond their understanding.

It was into their world in Laos that those early communist invaders went, back in 1953 and 1954. The purpose of the invasion-that-was-not-an-invasion was anything but inscrutable. Anyone who knew that those troops were backed by communist China understood that the purpose was to spread Chinese communism around Asia, and then around the world.

The 1953 expedition into Laos performed its task. It established a revolutionary government under communist Prince Souphanouvong in the town of Sam Neua. The 1954 invasion group spread the Prince's power into Phong Saly. In both these northern areas a political army was left behind, an army which immediately set up political schools. From these schools flying squads of organizers moved into the villages to start what are known today as Pathet Lao, or communist, cells. In doing this, the leaders of the Viet-Minh who defeated the French in Indo-China in 1954 simply used the experience gained in Indo-China.

Prince Souphanouvong began following the Chinese pattern in northern Laos in 1953 and 1954. The aim was to make those people in that town of Sam Neua deadly dangerous to us.

In May, 1958, in Vientiane, the government of Laos was shocked into drastic anticommunist measures. For the first time the government began to use some of the money received in American aid to do something for the farming people. The spark for this action came when communist Prince Souphanouvong, just taken into the Laotian government, emerged at the top of the list of *all* candidates running for government offices in the national elections. His Pathet Lao political party and its allies won thirteen of twenty-one seats in the new Parliament. Prince Souphanouvong was moving into a position in 1958 to finish part of Chapter Three in the Battle of Asia—legally—as the free choice of the Laotian people.

The shocked Laotian government saw what was happening, and that was the end of coalition government in Laos. The government saw what Chinese communist political organization could do and had done through trained specialists. By May, 1958, these specialists had set up communist cells in most of the villages of central and southern Laos, in addition to those in the north. Each cell was broken up into groups of five to ten families. Each cell met once every four or five days. At those meetings the people were told that the ruling government of Laos was the same small group of western-trained and western-educated men who had never done a thing for them. They learned that the money that came from America went into an army that existed to keep things as they were; an army the Laotian economy could not support. Every month the payroll for the entire Laotian army came from the United States. What was needed, the Pathet Lao spokesman said, was revolution:

"Throw the royal family out," he said. "You have a right to enough food, medical care, good housing, clothes, better tools and machines. We will get you these things."

By the time the elections of 1958 came along, political awareness was growing among war-weary Laotians. American arms and weapons did not impress them. These people saw and heard nothing about freedom and democracy as an alternative to communism. What they did see and what they did hear gave the communist Prince the greatest number of Laotian votes in May, 1958.

That May election, and the breakup of the Laotian coalition government immediately afterward, led directly to crisis in Laos. Prime Minister Phoumí Sananikone bought and passed out shovels and hoes by the thousands. He promised specific reforms, including better treatment for minorities in Laos.

If these reforms had worked, the Laotian story would be different today. If only the reforms had not been too little and too late. If only there were enough American pioneers willing to spend months away from the comforts of the capital city's hotels. If only they had the knowledge and the language ability to explain just how the things we say we believe might be used to do for Laos what these things have done for us. Then the explosion might have been averted. But to date, we are losing the Battle of Laos—Chapter Three in the story of the Battle of Asia.

The Battle of Africa is closely tied to the Battle of Asia. The headlines from the Congo and the other African countries shared space in the newspapers with the headlines from Laos and Viet-Nam. While two chapters of the Battle of Asia have been written, and both have marked defeat for the West, the story in Africa is not quite as bleak, because in Africa the Chinese brand of communism is not yet in ascendance.

Chapter One in the story of Africa was both a victory and a defeat. It concerned two African nations: Egypt and Tunisia. The United States thought Egypt and Syria were lost to communist infiltrators when Colonel Nasser threw off British dominance and, through an incredible series of western blunders, turned to Soviet Russia. But the Soviet Russians with their form of communism are really not much better geared than we are to dealing with the people of primitive society. The Russians think in terms of industrialization. That is how they acted in Egypt, where the fellaheen—the peasants—needed help in terms of that country's agricultural economy. We did not succeed in stopping the march of communism in Egypt. Rather, the Russians have been blundering badly where they held all the aces.

But Chapter One in the story of Africa ended with the emergence of nations which, unlike Egypt, had not even a pretense of national sovereignty in modern times. In Tunisia, where Habib Bourguiba's government at first seemed to enjoy ideal postwar relations with France, the first chapter in the Battle of Africa started off well for the West. At least so it seemed until Tunisian and French relations started to deteriorate. But in Morocco and Algeria matters took a turn for the worse. How? As far as Americans are concerned, the change began in 1944 and 1945 in the Moroccan city of Fez, and in the little Algerian town of Setif.

In North Central Morocco there has always been something special about the city of Fez. It is a holy place to the men of Mohammed. In January, 1944, fifty-seven leading Moslems of Morocco drafted a petition which they handed the French Governor-General in Fez, asking that some French ideas be made a reality for Moroccans. The French answer was what the Moroccans described afterward as a massacre. French troops fired into peaceful paraders who were carrying flags and banners that demanded "liberté, egalité, et fraternité."

The French had released those ideas into the world with their revolution 150 years earlier. At the end of World War II, at a critical time in French history, those ideas had been returned to them.

There's nothing special about the Algerian town of Setif. The American and British troops in Setif on liberty one weekend soon after V-E Day had no reason to expect anything special to happen there. What happened began as a parade by local Moslems who carried banners, and an old flag, and chanted slogans.

Suddenly the clamor, the peaceful clamor, was drowned out by the sound of gunfire. French troops, supported by tanks, moved in to break up the demonstration.

Algerians, too, described what happened that day as a massacre. Before it ended, forty-one Moslem villages and towns were wiped out, from Setif north to the Mediterranean Sea. A reliable report estimated the number killed at thirty-five thousand Moslem Algerians. This happened in an area where a particularly strong movement had developed during World War II to see those French ideas of liberty, equality and fraternity made a reality in Algeria.

What was the explanation for these events?

At the end of World War II, France was trying to become a great power again, trying to preserve its hold on North Africa, a prime source of French power before 1940. Since the war the communists have used two words with deadly effect against countries like France. The words are "colonialism" and "imperialism."

Most Americans have heard those words often enough, and are not particularly moved by Mr. Khrushchev's continual insistence on this theme. Like the Russians we sit very comfortably on rich lands. But for people like Moroccans and Algerians and most of the rest of the world, these are powerful words. Colonialism meant power for a poor France, when colonies like Indo-China, Guinea, the Gabon, Guiana, and others poured raw materials into France, then bought much of what France made of those materials. Breaking up the empire meant weakening such power. Mr. Khrushchev is obviously against colonialism because it means weakening that power, just as France was obviously for colonialism in order to maintain her old basis of power.

Now where is France? Morocco is no longer a colony. Tunisia is independent. Algeria is independent. Of all the parts of the old French empire, no area is more important to French power than these three countries in North Africa, but they are gone from France.

In July, 1961, when Tunisia tried to get France to leave the naval base at Bizerte, the French responded in fury, and the beginnings of a friendly relationship between France and Tunisia were wrecked. The Tunisians see the French hold on Bizerte as a last vestige of colonialism. Under the terms of their 1956 treaty with France they thought they would take the naval base over themselves one day. France cannot afford to give up this base. It is as important to France as Algeria was, because Bizerte defended the French lifeline of raw materials from Central Africa through to a French Algeria. Even if that lifeline could not be maintained, as now we see it could not, Bizerte was still vital to the defense of a different line. The second line was through the Mediterranean from West Africa, where French territory bordered on the Atlantic.

The growing animosity of Africa toward France is a vital problem for the United States, as well as for France, because we Americans are more deeply involved in the Battle of Africa than most of us realize.

There is a widespread feeling across North Africa that France would not have been able to wage war against the Algerian rebels if we had insisted that the French stop using the weapons they received from America. American weapons intended for use by France (as a member of the North Atlantic Treaty Organization) to defend Europe were being used against Algerian Moslems in a war that cost France one and one-half billion dollars a year. Rightly or wrongly, there are people all over North Africa, and all over Asia, who believe American money made that French war effort possible.

Nothing can be more dangerous to our future in Africa than that belief, because there are too many people around the world who dislike Americans. In Indonesia today, there are men and women who remember that their wives, husbands or brothers, or families were killed by American weapons in Dutch hands. In Indo-China there are people who had no love for communism but who remember bitterly that American arms in French hands helped kill their people not long ago.

France's problem in Algeria is listed on the French record as starting on the night of October 31, 1954. Actually, it goes back a long time before that, to a night in June, 1830, when a French army moved ashore at a place called Sidi Ferrouche. After twelve years of fighting France annexed Algeria, only to be faced finally with a revolt in that country where French-

men and Moslems have lived together and where the idea of
Algeria as a part of France was not questioned until the
1950s. What's more, the revolt was backed by what were supposed to be French Moslem *citizens*.

Why? Because for decades the Moslems were not citizens
at all.

Those early Frenchmen came ashore at Sidi Ferrouche with
the idea that Algerians were an inferior people. There is no
more dangerous way to deal with any group of human beings
on this planet today. Until very recently, the French said
Algerians were "uneducable"—impossible to educate.

What those Frenchmen did not know was that North Africans, like the Algerians, were descendants of peoples who had
started the Romans down the road to history's junk heap. Back
in the Fourth Century, they pushed the Romans out of Africa.
On donkeys and in war chariots, in that terrain the Romans
were no match for camel-mounted North Africans. And in
our time Frenchmen, standing among ruined villages, trying
to flush out Algerian rebels to force French law and culture
on North Africans, tried to do exactly what the Roman Augus-
tus and his Third Legion tried to do to enforce the *Pax Ro-
mana*. The ancestors of those Algerians put an end to Rome
in North Africa, and now some of their descendants have
repeated that bit of history with the French.

But France, though now by more enlightened methods, is
still determined to hold power in at least part of Algeria. Oil
is the reason. Oil found in the last few years in the Sahara in
places like Hassi Messaoud. This place boasts little more than
an oil pool about five hundred feet deep, but it ranks with the
most important sources of oil in the Middle East. The trouble
is, Hassi Messaoud lies in disputed Sahara territory, and Tunisia, the Algerian nationalists, and other neighboring countries have all laid claim to parts of the Sahara.

There are other valuable properties in Algeria. In what was
considered only a few years ago to be useless desert waste-

land, French prospectors, and Americans, and others have found large amounts of iron, manganese, copper and natural gas. But finding these resources, and developing them so that they can be used in the French economy, are two very different things.

France is not a very big country. Its national income is not large. France does not have the money to stand the continued expense of developing oil fields and ore bodies alone. When the first oil strikes were made in the Saharan oil fields, there were only seventy drilling rigs, with trained crews qualified to run them, in all of the French territories; and they weren't all sitting in the Sahara.

To handle the exploration of the Saharan fields and what is left of French holdings in Africa, France hoped to be able to put down four hundred wells immediately. This meant adding at least a thousand more trained specialists to the crews then working, and buying the extra oil rigs.

French universities and training schools were equipped to turn out about one hundred and fifty such oilmen a year. To buy the oil rigs from anyone else would have meant using money badly needed elsewhere. The only answer was to let out part of the job to Americans, Canadians, Germans, and Italians, and for these people to develop French African resources together. That is what happened.

Most Americans have never heard of the town of Moanda, or for that matter of a land called the Gabon, just off the Congo Republic in the bend of Africa. Moanda, in the Gabon, is a more important town to us than it is to France because of manganese, its chief product. Manganese is why our United States Steel Company has a 49 per cent share in the company that U. S. Steel helped to build there. We turn out about two hundred and thirty thousand tons of manganese from our own mines, but we use over one million six hundred thousand tons of manganese each year to make high-grade steels. We need manganese as much as France does. That is why we helped stake out and develop one of the biggest manganese strikes in recent history. The reserves at Moanda are as good as the Soviet Union's reserves, which were earlier considered to be the best in the world. Moanda is an important place name in our affairs.

Another important place name to Americans, also in the Gabon, is Mekambo, where iron ores were found comparable in quality to our Mesabi iron ores in Minnesota. Our history would not have been the same without that easily mined high-grade Mesabi deposit, but it is nearly used up. That is why the Bethlehem Steel Corporation has a 55 per cent share in Mekambo. And there are other names just as important—Franceville, Edjele, and Libreville—where uranium, oil, and potassium have been found. Much of Africa, not just French Africa, was vital to the power of the Roman Empire once. All of Africa is vital to the power of Europe and the Americas today.

All of which are the ingredients of the history that will be written in the Battle of Africa. The key lies among the people of Africa who in the northern, central, or southern parts, whatever the color of their skins, are demanding for themselves exactly what those paraders in Setif and Fez wanted at the end of World War II. In the days of colonialism and imperialism, most of the peoples of the colonized countries benefited very little from their being part of an empire. Today, the overwhelming majority of these peoples are convinced that the French, and others like them, are powerful and wealthy because the colonies were milked dry.

The student in French West Africa, for example, knows that before World War II a Frenchman consumed an average of thirteen pounds of fats and oils each year, while West Africans who provided much of that oil from palm and peanuts were getting by on six pounds apiece. After World War II, the French announced plans to triple the output of fats and oils in their African colonies to about nine hundred and forty thousand tons a year. Of that amount, eight hundred and eighty thousand tons was to be exported to France and only sixty thousand tons was to be left to the colonies. It is this kind of economy that Algerians fought against, and that Moroccans fought against, and that the whole colonial world has rebelled against since World War II.

Colonialism and imperialism are dead issues, whether France and the other powers acknowledge it or not. France was slow to accept this fact. The concessions France offered French Algeria came too late, just as French concessions came too late in Indo-China. In many ways, the problems of Africa and the problems of Asia are the same. In many ways, the battles are being fought on the same lines. This is particularly true since Red China has entered the fight in Africa, trying to persuade the Africans to accept—not just communism—but *Chinese* communism, which, in Africa, would be a much greater danger to the western world than Russian communism.

We are fighting the second phase in the Battle of Africa, and the third phase in the Battle of Asia, as these words are written. Everywhere, the struggle is on the same basic grounds: the demand of poor people to enter the Twentieth Century. The battles are joined.

Are half measures enough to keep our children secure from communism? Will bullets and bayonets answer the questions about better lives that Laotians are asking today, after having been worked over for years by the communists to make them aware of such things?

Ninety billion dollars poured into half measures since the end of World War II have done no more than delay the spread of communism. Three hundred million dollars in American arms in Laos have not killed a single communist idea. Arms can kill people but not ideas.

We did not win World War II with half measures and wrong measures. We cannot win a free future for the world today with half measures or wrong measures, either. No formula, no new answer is needed to do what has to be done. You with full stomachs must make the effort to understand the needs and wants of people with empty stomachs. You with warm homes must know the problems of people with no homes. You with healthy bodies must know the problems of people with sick ones. Why? Because today your freedom is indivisible from the problems of hunger, health, and housing. The opportunity to enjoy freedom will end for you unless it exists for the poor of the world.

CHAPTER 5

Brain Power—I

NOT LONG AGO, a teacher in a small town in Minnesota was suspended by his school superintendent for assigning his high school students a book called *1984*, a classic political satire by the late George Orwell. This book is a fictional story about some future Britain, after that country lost sight of its traditions and turned into a kind of super-technocracy by the year 1984.

That apparently unimportant incident concerning a teacher in Minnesota touches an important problem in American education. A problem that was exposed even as the nation breathed a sigh of relief as the Korean War ended in 1953.

With the prisoner exchange at Panmunjom, Korea, as the nation saw it then, war had ended and another problem was solved.

It was not long after the prisoners returned home that the nation learned that the end of the Korean War was not the end of a problem, but the beginning of one.

78

We knew that American prisoners of war had marched in demonstrations against what the Chinese communists described as "American aggression" and "American imperialism." It was taken for granted at the time that those American prisoners were forced to do so, that they faced torture or death if they did not. The nation sympathized. This was a consoling explanation for the public at that time. For the most part that story stands, because the public was not told too much about communist Chinese papers which fell into our hands several months before the Korean fighting ended.

Those papers told a disturbing story about Chinese communist success in indoctrinating American prisoners of war.

Americans participated in parades. Some made propaganda broadcasts. Some signed peace petitions, and even confessed to carrying on germ warfare and worse. They were under *no* threat of torture, *no* threat of death!

This story disturbed military people so much that they decided to look into it. So did a special Congressional committee.

The Army's tape recordings of interviews with Americans who were prisoners of war in Korea have never been played for the nation, but a special report of the Congressional Committee on the American Prisoner of War can be read by the public. Further, a book on the subject was later published. It was called *In Every War But One*.

This book is the story of the American prisoner of war in Korea, and it concludes that our educational system failed to give those prisoners of war, and other young people of this nation, any real understanding of the American heritage, or American history, or American democracy.

The Korean War revealed a dangerous lack of loyalty to this country, an almost complete ignorance about the political, social, economic, and religious facts of American life. And the reports revealed an absolute ignorance about communism, the enemy those youngsters went to Korea to fight. The young Americans captured in Korea were unable to defend their faith and their belief in democracy against the arguments of their communist captors because they knew nothing about the communists or their philosophy.

As a former university teacher, I know some of the reasons why America's educational system did not prepare young Americans to defend their faith, and their way of life, in communist prisoner-of-war camps.

For the most part, your American educational system is still not doing this job. The attitude of that Minnesota school superintendent is part of the "reason why." So are some other actions by adult and apparently intelligent Americans which have been reported from time to time in the postwar years.

Do you know that in 1959 the Missouri Legislature spent many hours debating a bill which would make it a crime to teach Darwin's theory of evolution in Missouri's schools? This happened thirty-five years after the Scopes Trial had made headlines on the same matter in Tennessee.

Evolution lost the fight in Tennessee thirty-five years ago. Tennessee still restricts what can be taught about evolution. Arkansas has similar laws, and last year pressure groups in Missouri wanted to pass laws which would restrict what young Americans there could learn about evolution.

Do you know that in Southern California a teacher can get into very serious trouble now by discussing the work of the United Nations Educational, Scientific and Cultural Organization? Pressure groups have succeeded in restricting what young Americans in California can learn about the United Nations and its work.

Not long ago in Evanston, Illinois, there was a vicious fight between local "patriotic" groups and the school board over the use of a high school textbook which included a chapter about communism and how it worked. Nobody won that fight.

In the light of these examples, it would be very interesting to know how many young Americans in Chinese-operated prison camps in Korea came from schools where education was degutted and deboned of meaning: where education was restricted to conform to the prejudices of minority pressure groups. Such education does not prepare young Americans to fight either a hot war with Korean and Chinese communists, or the more important cold war they must fight today.

According to our Voice of America broadcasts to communist countries, only under a democratic form of government is it possible for people to govern themselves. Only in a democracy is there equal opportunity and justice for all people before the law, regardless of race, creed or religion. Only under the rules of a democracy is government kept from violating personal rights and personal privacy. Censorship of the news, of books, and of films is not approved here. Freedom of speech and freedom of assembly for all peoples exist here. Only in a democracy, we say to the world, does labor have the right to strike for its rights. These things set our way of life apart from the ways of people who live under military dictatorships, under communism, under socialism, or any kind of totalitarianism.

That is what your government *says*. But how do our young people in American classrooms feel about the points covered in those Voice of America broadcasts to Russians and Hungarians and Czechs and Poles, and to others behind the Iron Curtain?

For seventeen years the Remmers testing group at Purdue University has been checking opinions of teen-agers in high schools across the nation. The last results show that half of three thousand students chosen by sampling did not believe that most people are capable of governing themselves.

More than half of these youngsters in our classrooms favored censorship of books, magazines, newspapers, radio, and televison. More than half of them believed that the police should use force, that is, the third degree, and that people who refuse to testify against themselves should be forced to do so, whether or not it violates personal rights, and no matter that the Constitution expressly forbids it.

Almost 60 per cent of these students either were not sure whether labor should be allowed to strike for its rights, or they were opposed to the right to strike. Almost half did not approve, or were not sure about allowing freedom of speech and assembly to all groups.

Statements about our democratic principles in those Voice of America broadcasts simply are not supported by most of tomorrow's caretakers and defenders of the American heritage, at least according to the Remmers tests.

Those student answers show that at the very least there is confusion about democracy—the same kind of confusion that kept those Korean War prisoners from defending their faith and belief in their American heritage. They did not know their heritage. They did not know because an important part of that heritage has been lost, and lost in our time. The lost heritage includes the most important of all rights in a democracy, the right to know. And this includes the right to know Darwin's theory of evolution, the workings of the United Nations Educational and Scientific Organization, and the workings of communism—among other things.

Anyone who has written a textbook for use in our schools today, particularly for use in what are called the social sciences, knows how hard it is to put anything meaningful into it without antagonizing someone. Our schools are supersensitive to any kind of criticism. Generally they yield to every pressure group. The result is that most school textbooks have little or no substance. Our classes bypass controversy, barely considering the basic political, social, economic, and religious problems of our time.

So American students, by and large, are not prepared to meet the problems of our time. Our young people do not understand what democracy means, what it takes to make it work, and what it takes to defend it.

All of this has been discussed year after year in the conventions of the National School Board Associations. During the very week that a group tried to restrict the right of young Missourians to know the widest range of things, speakers at the NSBA convention urged the nation's school administrators to try to get more meat into courses, and to put controversial issues back into the classrooms of the nation. They knew that today's crop of pallid and meatless subjects in our schools can not possibly prepare tomorrow's Americans to live in a world of controversy. Those speakers asked that the right to know be given back to our young people to prevent the loss of freedom and democracy at home, as well as in the rest of the world.

When James Madison was the fourth President of the United States, he faced this issue and dealt with it squarely. Popular government, President Madison said, is impossible without popular knowledge. And by "popular" he meant the widest possible range of knowledge; not restricted, not blocked by the prejudices and fears and ignorance of the few. This kind of knowledge would have helped young Americans live up to their heritage in those Korean prisoner-of-war camps.

And what of the rest of the world? In Asia, in the Middle East, in Africa, in South and Central America, there democracy has failed, time and again. Most alarming is the failure of democracy in the new nations of the world.

People in these new nations have just emerged from colonialism. They have tried democracy, or what they thought was democracy, and they have discarded it in favor of other systems. It happened in Indonesia. It happened in Turkey. It happened in Iraq, in Pakistan, in Thailand, in Burma, in Lebanon, and in the Sudan.

The fact is that except for three lands—India, the Philippines, and Israel—what can be called democracy has not worked in the lands that have become independent since 1945.

The unhappy results of this failure are apparent all over the world. It is apparent today in Africa, that huge continent which is dividing so quickly into nations, that the peoples there are inclined toward other systems. They have seen "democracy." They are not impressed.

Most of us do not understand why all this has happened. For the most part, we have taken it for granted that once any people anywhere had independence, they would choose the way of freedom and democracy, because ours is obviously the best of all ways of life on earth.

There is not much doubt that our way of life is good. There is not much doubt that it has provided considerable happiness for most of us. Yet there really is some question as to whether anybody else on this planet can follow our example, to become what we are.

I remember a statement about this which appeared in a textbook that I used in my college classes several years ago.

Freedom and democracy, said this book, were the natural states of men; all other states of men were not natural.

In the light of history that statement is pure bunk!

Human history makes it clear that freedom and democracy are unusual states of mankind. They are anything but natural. They are unique, in fact. Our American contribution to human history came when the Pinckneys and the Hamiltons, the Washingtons and the Livingstons, the Shermans and the Jeffersons turned their backs on a world in which tyranny, inequality, injustice, and servitude were the natural states of men.

Well, those early Americans laid out a different state for men. Today's Americans, young or old, who do not understand this fact about the American heritage cannot possibly help other people to understand and make use of it. In fact, we did not help those short-lived democracies at all.

It is important to understand that there is absolutely nothing about Americans as human beings to explain our political, social and economic development. We do not have superior brains. We do not have superior bodies. But we do have a very special history.

At any point in that history, something could have happened to make this American story of ours very different.

Take a point anywhere in the last four thousand years, and suppose at that point events had been different. Choose a point in the late Thirteenth Century, in England, where a law was passed, the Statute of Westminster Second. That law had to do with a revolution. Many of our history books do not mention it, but had it not happened the American story would have been a different one.

What was that statute? It was a law that recognized the right of men to hold private property. That idea spread across Europe in a few hundred years. From Europe it spread to the colonies of North America, where farmers set up single family farms. The existence of those farms, in turn, made possible for us the freedom and democracy we now enjoy.

Thomas Jefferson said that America's political democracy was one of the products of those family farms. He was aware of the unique nature of the experiment in America: the idea that ordinary men, lowborn men, not kings, not princes, not sultans, not barons, but just plain men, could own land in their own names and work it for their own private benefit.

That Statute of Westminster Second is *not* part of the history of the Iraqis, the Pakistanis, the Burmese, or the Sudanese.

That revolution—land reform—has not yet reached most of the world.

Or, take another important point in history, again in the Thirteenth Century, and again in England. At Runnymede, a group of English aristocrats squeezed a political paper about human rights out of their king. You know that paper as the *Magna Charta*. No such historical accident happened to give landless peasants in Iraq, Pakistan, Burma or the rest of those short-lived democracies the political ideas that led to our way of life. Each of those places had the form of democracy; they had parliaments, they had prime ministers, and they had presidents. But they had no roots like the Magna Charta or the Statute of Westminster Second, or any of the many, many, many others.

The Magna Charta was particularly important to us because it changed England into a nation based on laws instead of regal whims. The descendants of those Englishmen one day sailed to North America taking with them this idea of a nation based on laws. We have been trying to make that idea work as the support of freedom and democracy ever since.

But it is a point that has not been settled yet, as anyone knows who is familiar with the continuing squabble over Supreme Court decisions. Most certainly it is a point that was never settled for the people of those short-lived democracies where that kind of law never existed.

These are facts. In today's kind of world they are critically important facts, without which no American is prepared to defend his faith and belief in his way of life against any kind of attack; without which no American is prepared to help any people anywhere to develop our ideas into their ways of life; without which no American is prepared to make freedom and democracy work for us at home.

"Fact" and "prepared": two very important words, because they stress the most important fact of all in today's kind of world—the fact that the future belongs to whoever prepares for it best.

CHAPTER 6

Brain Power—II

THE MOST POWERFUL man on earth today heads no government, he runs no army, and most Americans have never heard of him. His name, Mstislav V. Keldysh, is recognized only by a very few people around the world despite the fact that in our time no man is in a position to do more to change the lives of as many people around the world.

Keldysh is a powerful man, with a big job to do. He is the present head of the Academy of Sciences of the Soviet Union. His job is to change the world: to change its politics, its economics, even its appearance in order to insure a certain kind of future for the whole human race. Keldysh's job is a big one, but not exactly a new one. Any good world history book will make it very clear that other men have tried to do the same, many times before.

The first such attempt undoubtedly was made in the day of Og the caveman. The Emperor Nebuchadnezzar tried to change the world in his day. Alexander the Great, Genghis Khan, and Adolf Hitler tried it. For the most part, from Og the caveman to Adolf the Nazi, those men failed. But they did not have the tools that are available to Keldysh.

In the early 1950s, the former head of the Academy of Sciences, Alexander Nesmeyanov, began to put those tools to work. One day he signed an order to develop large-scale production of a new kind of fuel, a high-energy fuel, for a completely new kind of motive power. That order was the first step to a new kind of transportation to power satellites and men into outer space. The world, its politics, economics, science, and technology, has not been the same since that order was carried out.

During the late 1950s Alexander Nesmeyanov issued another important order, a directive ordering Soviet scientists to develop an incident solar absorber: a machine to change sunlight into usable energy. If successful, it will be a completely different kind of sun-powered generator from what has been worked out anywhere on earth. If this order is carried out, it means the Russians will have perfected a source of cheap power wherever there is sunlight. This development alone can change the world's industry, shaking the world's politics and economics to their roots.

On Keldysh's desk are other plans and orders. They add up to a blueprint for a world you would scarcely recognize, a world, for example, that would no longer contain a Mediterranean Sea. One plan on his desk calls for a dam eight miles long at the Strait of Gibraltar between Africa and Spain, to separate the Atlantic and the Mediterranean. In this way, thousands of miles of fertile land now covered by Mediterranean salt water could be drained and turned over to the exploding populations of Africa and the Middle East. In that changed world another dam would shift the warm Japanese Sea currents into the cold Sea of Okhotsk off the western coast of North Asia, changing the climate of the Far East and of the whole Northern Hemisphere.

In that changed world, most of the Sahara Desert would be wiped out. Low spots like the Qattara and Bodélé depressions in Egypt and Chad, respectively, would be filled with fresh-water lakes. All over the world, automobiles, airplanes and factories would be run by "broadcast power," by energy trans-mitted to motors the way radio waves are transmitted to radio and television sets.

Does all that seem fantastic, impractical, improbable, fool-ish? If you think so you do not live in the world of Mistislav V. Keldysh, and the more than one hundred thousand people who take directions from that office on the second floor of the building at 14 Leninski Lane in Moscow. Keldysh and his predecessors in office have been the real power behind the drive of the Khrushchevs, Suslovs, Mikoyans, and Malenkovs to see a changed world, a communist world for the whole human race.

The important difference with the past is that Keldysh is using a new basis of power to try to change the world.

If you had been along on the eighty-four-day underwater trip around the world of the American atom-powered sub-marine *Triton,* in 1960, one day you would have seen the skipper raise a periscope in Philippine waters, a hundred feet away from a Filipino fisherman. The fisherman did not know a submarine was there. While the *Triton* was only a hundred feet away from him in space, it was, in fact, hundreds of years away from him in time. That American naval officer looked out of the age of science through his periscope, back through time to the much earlier agricultural age of the Filipino fisher-man in his dugout canoe.

That globe-circling machine, the atomic submarine, was the result of a way of thinking that the Filipino and most of the human race know little or nothing about. The submarine was the result of the science of cryogenics, of solid-state physics, theoretical mathematics, geomagnetics, atomic physics, atomic chemistry, geophysics, oceanography, geodetics, hydraulics, and statics, to mention only a few of the sciences involved. These sciences are part of the everyday lives of all Americans and they are understood by all Americans. All Americans know that those sciences serve as the basis for the kind of thinking Americans do, and the kind of political and economic actions Americans take to solve their problems in the age of science. On the other hand, most Filipinos, Burmese, Hottentots, Bolivian Indians, Indian Indians, Eskimos, and Afghans know little or nothing of these sciences. Most of them, and most of the world, still believe the earth is the center of the universe, and that the sun and stars revolve around the earth. Most of those people believe the world is flat. Where the idea of a round world has penetrated, there is little or no idea about how large the world is. For most of the world, our science is a good deal like their magic: mysterious and possibly evil. They are a bit fearful of it.

Americans, of course, know better, and nothing sets the world of the *Triton* atomic submarine apart so much from the world of that Filipino fisherman as the fact that all Americans do know better and understand all about the science and technology that make our way of life possible: from cryogenics to statics. We understand science, and we respect it. Of course we do. Of course.

In Chapter Five, I mentioned some interesting facts about the attitudes of young Americans toward freedom. They were shocking attitudes about political, economic, and religious matters, but equally shocking are the attitudes of American teen-agers toward science, as shown by that same Remmers testing group at Purdue University.

In 1957, the Remmers group set out to discover what young people in high schools around the nation know about science in the age of science, and what they think about it. They found that over 40 per cent of the youngsters questioned either believed the earth was the center of the universe, or were not sure about its place. Almost 65 per cent believed the circumference of the earth was 125,000 miles. More than a third of those high school youngsters found the subjects taught in science "boring." A quarter of those questioned thought scientists as a group were "weird." Most of these youngsters believed scientists were radicals of the Fu Manchu type who did not care about the effects of their work on people. Almost 70 per cent of the high-schoolers questioned across the nation said they would not like to be scientists. They felt there was something about science that was mysterious and possibly evil. They were a bit fearful of it.

In other words, no small number of young Americans right now are actually just about where that young Filipino fisherman was as he stared into the *Triton's* periscope: roughly two thousand years behind the Age of Science. Significantly, that Remmers report was released in October, 1957, the month a Soviet rocket placed the first man-made satellite in space.

That Soviet rocket came out of the research laboratories, institutes of theoretical and applied sciences, and classrooms run by, or influenced by, the Soviet Academy of Science. It is the product of the Age of Science that very few Americans really understand or respect. This fact makes Mistislav Keldysh one of the most serious threats to our future that we have faced in all the time we have been a political democracy. The average Russian knows less about science than the average American, but men like Nesmeyanov and Keldysh do not need the approval of the Soviet citizen to order their jobs done. The Soviet citizen's vote has no effect on what the Soviet Academy of Sciences does to develop Russia's scientific and technological power. But American scientists do need the approval of American citizens to develop America's scientific and technological power. What the American citizen thinks has a great effect on the kind of research and development our scientists do, because as the American thinks, he buys, and he votes. What he thinks about wrap-around windshields on his cars, about colored telephones, and about dishwashers and electric can openers, explains why most American scientific talent and research outside government has not gone into developing new fuels, and new kinds of motive power from new sources of energy.

We have some of the finest automobiles, ballpoint pens and refrigerators in the world, but even the most remarkable future invention in automobiles, ballpoint pens, or refrigerators will hardly keep the world from being changed Keldysh's way. New sources of energy to make industry possible, development of "broadcast" power, draining oceans, and changing climates can change the world Keldysh's way, not ours.

Leadership in science, in the Age of Science, is the road Mistislav Keldysh is traveling to make sure that the future will belong to the communists. The ignorance of science expressed by young Americans in that Remmers survey, and the even greater ignorance among older, voting Americans, is the surest and quickest way by which we can give the future to the communists. Because we are citizens of a democracy, and we have responsibilities that are not being met.

One of the oldest lessons of history, and easily the hardest to learn, is that whatever else change may be, it is inevitable. Man undoubtedly first faced this problem perhaps five hundred thousand years ago. For years Og the caveman had been satisfied with a way of life based on his stone tools and stone weapons, but one day a stranger appeared with a bow and arrow. Against this new power, this new way of doing things, Og was almost defenseless with his Stone Age tools and weapons. What he did then has become one of the oldest lessons in history. In order to survive, Og gave up his old, comfortable way of doing things and learned to use the bow and arrow.

Considerably later, Ab, the early hunter, found life pleasant and agreeable with the bow and arrow way of life, until one day he faced an enemy armed with tools and weapons made of metal. To survive, Ab gave up the bow and arrow, dressed in armor and learned to use metal tools and weapons.

For Fauntleroy, the English knight, the metal, armored way of life was pleasant and comfortable until, in a battle fought in Normandy, French troops using two primitive cannons killed and injured five thousand six hundred Englishmen, while losing only twelve of their own men. Englishmen lost no time in tossing out their comfortable ideas. They shifted to cannon power.

We won World War II as the greatest power in the Industrial Age, but today's world has shifted to a new age. It shifted in October, 1957, when the first Russian Sputnik went into orbit. We are now where Og, and Ab, and Fauntleroy were before us. What do we do? In our case, as in theirs, survival is at stake. Bigger and better cars, ballpoint pens, and handsome refrigerators are no longer any guarantee of the "good life." Mistislav Keldysh and those who went before him have changed the picture. They represent the Age of Science.

In all this, the lesson of history for us is that no people, anywhere on earth, at any time, have ever been able to live out their lives on their own terms, no matter how good those terms were, or how much they preferred them.

This touches on an interesting and revealing incident that occurred not too long ago at a well-known university. It happened just after the final examination period, when an honors committee met to decide which students would graduate with distinction. The committee was made up of twelve men. Four were professors from the departments of the social sciences; four were professors from the departments of humanities; four were professors from the departments of the physical sciences.

The papers of the top students were passed out and examined. Suddenly one of the professors from the humanities leaned back in his chair and laughed. He turned to the other men sitting around the table, showed them one particular paper, and made a remark about it which brought down the house. All twelve men found something about that paper to be very funny. All laughed and then they got back to business.

Sometime later another professor, this time from the physics department, leaned back in his chair, smiled and made a remark about one of his papers. This time the house did not come down. Only three other men at that table saw anything funny in the physics professor's remark. The rest smiled politely, looked puzzled, and then got back to business.

Those incidents meant that two students did not graduate with honors that day. But indirectly, they also meant that one of the places to begin tackling the deep-seated and widespread ignorance about science that exists in this country right now is in the training of the people who become teachers.

The remark made by the humanities professor that brought down the house concerned a paper turned in by a student named Cicero Amatrido. Cicero failed to get a high grade in Latin. That seemed funny, Cicero not doing well in Latin, because during the time of the Roman Empire, Marcus Tullius Cicero (about 106 to 43 B.C.) was the greatest of all Roman orators and writers. Naturally he wrote and spoke Latin. No one at that faculty table could pretend to be a cultured person unless he knew this, whether he was physicist or philosopher, linguist or biologist. Cicero got a good laugh.

But there was no general laughter at the remark made by the physics professor that a student named Gauss had failed to get a proper grade for honors in mathematics. Everyone knows who Cicero was, but who was Gauss? Well, Karl Friedrich Gauss, born in 1777, in Germany, was one of the three or four really great mathematicians in history. His work paved the way to the science and technology that led directly to the Soviet and American space satellites today.

Only the men from the science departments of the university knew about this man. Eight of the twelve men sitting around that table were not well-rounded men. They were cultured and educated men, suited to the world of 1900, but not equipped for the world of the 1960s.

A knowledge of Keats, Victor Hugo and Goethe, a smattering of French and German, and a passing acquaintance with music and the arts may have been the measure of the cultured man yesterday when culture did not include the ninhydrin stained finger or the smell of hydrogen sulfide. There was no disgrace in not knowing about such things in the industrial age. There was no danger in not knowing the difference between an electron and a proton.

Today there is a danger. Since October 4, 1957, Karl Friedrich Gauss, those who went before him, and those who came after him in science have come into their own. Man is racing for outer space, riding electrons and protons and the results of work in cryogenics, geodetics, solid-state physics, statics, astrophysics, space mechanics, and the rest of the sciences. Our schools and universities have a vital job to do if we are to be up front in that race, and not to fall farther and farther behind. Our educators need to look hard at just what it takes to be a well-rounded person in the Age of Science.

The first thing it takes is the well-rounded teacher. There is a direct line from the teacher who understands the Age of Science to students who understand it. There is another line too, just as direct: the line from a public that understands the Age of Science to teachers who understand it. The latter is the more important of the two lines, but it does not exist today.

A year after Nesmeyanov and his Soviet Academy of Science put Sputnik I into space, a report came from our National Science Foundation about what we had done through our schools to counter Nesmeyanov's effort to lead the world to a communist future. Very little had been done, said that report, largely because the parents of American schoolchildren showed no real concern over the problem. Without public support for changes in the American classroom, little could be done. That 1958 report ended by saying that the public was very poorly informed about our problems in the Age of Science. That report urged that something be done.

Since 1958 there have been other reports on the subject. Three years after Sputnik the public was still poorly informed about science age problems, despite the fact that the shelves in our libraries and bookstores across the country are crammed with books about those problems written since the first Sputnik. For some reason those books do not sell or circulate as well as the paperback murder, mayhem, and mystery stories do. Magazines have published hundreds of articles, month after month, about those problems, but for some reason those magazines do not sell as well as the love story and movie magazines do. There are newspapers which treat those problems day after day, but for some reason their circulation is small, compared with the newspapers that follow the happenings in bedrooms and brothels around the world. There has been television coverage and radio coverage of those science age problems, but for some reason their ratings do not compare with those for the dance bands, unspeakables, or the cockeyed version of American history called "westerns."

It is just possible that the part of the public described in the National Science Foundation report in 1958 as "poorly informed" about problems affecting our future as a free people, simply does not know what earlier Americans meant by the word "freedom." Freedom was not a gift. Earlier Americans worked hard for it. The heart of the American story, into our own time, is just such problems faced and solved.

CHAPTER 7

Secrecy, Censorship, and Survival

THE POINT HAS BEEN MADE that education, modern, scientific education, is essential for the survival of our freedom. Americans cannot be a free people unless they can compete with the Soviet Union's scientific advances, and with the *use* of those advances for broad social purposes, from building dams to changing of the faces of seas and continents.

In considering the problems of education and of science, however, Americans must face another problem of their own making, the problem of secrecy and censorship. This, again, results from our deficiencies in education about the ways, and problems, and substance of science. This was made painfully clear during a meeting of British and American scientists sometime in the late 1940s.

They met during the research that was then going on to produce the hydrogen bomb. The purpose of that meeting was to deal with a problem that was serious then, and is serious now.

97

With the exception of one scientist at that meeting, they all agreed about how that problem should be handled. That lone dissenting British scientist was Klaus Fuchs, a name that is now infamous in the Western world.

Klaus Fuchs was the German-born British scientist who fed his knowledge of the atomic bomb to the Russians in the years when the British and American governments were trying desperately to retain atomic secrets. Few Americans or Britons, however, know that among the scientists who worked on the atomic bomb, one of the handful who *favored secrecy* in atomic affairs was that same Klaus Fuchs.

Until 1950, Fuchs was head of the theoretical physics department at Harwell, Britain's leading atomic research center. He had good reason to be pleased that so many highly placed political people in America agreed with him. They also urged that there should not be a free exchange of atomic information among the scientists of the non-communist world. His reason was made quite clear when, in 1950, he was arrested by the British for having given the scientists of the communist world the same secrets that he said should not be given to the scientists of the free world.

As a trained scientist sympathetic to the goals and interests of the U.S.S.R., Dr. Fuchs knew what interference in the free exchange of scientific information in the non-communist world would mean, sooner or later. He knew what scientifically illiterate American politicians did not know: that there is no such thing as a "secret" in science. All secrets can be worked out by qualified persons.

In the hands of Americans who do not know this, a rubber stamp marked "secret" can become the deadliest weapon in the world—one that *we* wield against *ourselves*.

To support this point, consider what happened in 1946, when two scientists working in completely unrelated fields met at a scientific meeting. In talking about their work and their problems they made an interesting discovery. One man was

doing research in atomic energy. The other was an archeologist, who spent his time digging up old bones, baskets, and
pots of early man. The archeologist's problem was to date those
bones, baskets, and pots accurately.

The physicist said he thought he might have an answer to
that problem. He explained to the archeologist that all living
things become slightly radioactive during their lifetime, from
radiation that gets through the earth's atmosphere from outer
space, or from the earth itself. When that plant or animal dies,
the radioactivity lasts a long time and diminishes at a fixed,
known rate.

The physicist arranged with that archeologist to bring some
of those bones, baskets, and pots into his laboratory to measure
the amount of radioactivity left in them. They could then fix
the point in time of the material used in making the baskets
and pots, and the people or animals that left the bones. The
archeologist did this and on that day a new field of science was
born: carbon 14 dating.

Now this happened by chance, in a free discussion by two
scientists about their work. That kind of discussion could not
take place freely in this country today because of security
restrictions. Most of the great developments in science happened just this way—by chance—without man's knowing what
to look for, just by sharing ideas in science.

The British and American scientists meeting in the late 1940s
all knew that this was at the heart of progress in science. Dr.
Klaus Fuchs knew this too. That was why Dr. Fuchs voted to
keep that block there, to slow down scientific progress in the
non-communist countries, so that one day when man made
his first move into space it would be in a Soviet, not an American, rocket and satellite; and so that when man made his
first trip into space, it would be a Soviet, not an American,
astronaut who made the trip. And this is exactly what happened.

The block is still with us: secrecy in science. It is the greatest single threat to our future as a leading scientific power in the world.

All this should have been clear in 1949. The nation had been assured by the highest authorities that under the best of conditions, the Russians might just possibly devise an A-bomb by 1954 or 1955, at the earliest. There were a considerable number of experts who were sure it would not happen for at least twenty years. After all, we had taken many precautions to see to it that it would not happen.

We continued to stamp everything we knew about atom bombs "Top Secret," but somehow, despite this, one September day in 1949, not 1955, at one of its atomic testing grounds, the U.S.S.R. became an atomic power—surprising and shocking our nation and most of the experts.

Not all Americans were shocked by this event, however.

On September 21, 1945, eleven men were gathered together with the President of the United States to make a very important decision. One of those men was Henry L. Stimson, Secretary of War under Presidents Roosevelt and Truman, who knew about this country's "Top Secret" development of the atomic bomb.

He knew how the bomb had been developed by bringing to this country the knowledge of many scientists in many places; how they turned out the miracle of atomic energy in 1945. It was a miracle of minds, the minds of Einstein, Meitner, Frisch, Hahn, and Strassman—all from Germany. They worked with the ideas of Curie and Joliot—Frenchmen; Bohr—a Dane; Fermi—an Italian; Ramsey, Rutherford, and Chadwick—Englishmen; and those of Anderson, Lawrence, and Oppenheimer —Americans.

These names are important, particularly important for Americans to hear and know because far too many people in this country do not know that the atomic bomb was not purely an American invention, but the result of international effort and international science.

Henry L. Stimson knew this. He knew that to any trained scientific mind, the theory and principle of atomic energy were not secrets. He tried to tell the other members of that Truman Cabinet what he knew, but he failed.

Because he failed that day, September 21, 1945, was a fateful day in American history. Mr. Stimson told President Truman that all the top scientists he had worked with were convinced that there was no possible way to keep the scientific facts about atomic energy and the bomb secret. It was his opinion that there should be a free exchange of atomic energy information with all interested countries in the United Nations.

Only one of the ten Cabinet members at that meeting had enough background in science to understand what Stimson was talking about. The rest were as ignorant about the science that made atomic energy possible as was the man on the street. Like the man on the street, they could not believe Stimson's statement that there were no basic, theoretical secrets involved. And because of this, they decided to set up an American monopoly of atomic energy. President Truman informed the world of this a few weeks later. He said we would keep, as a sacred trust, our secrets about the bomb.

Because atomic energy has been used for more than bombs since 1945—in medicine, metallurgy, power production, electronics, food production—that secret label on atomic energy has now spread into parts of our lives undreamed of on that day back in 1945. That day our nation changed from one in which open government and open science had been the rule, to today's closed kind, closed by the restriction of secrecy. Since that day, we have lived with the "secret" stamp. But secrecy has not worked because secrecy could not work.

One of the reasons it could not work is clear from a ceremony that took place at the Franklin Institute in Philadelphia in 1944. That institute is one of our top scientific centers but the ceremony rated no headlines. There did not seem to be anything especially exciting about a Russian scientist named

Dr. Peter Kapitza being awarded one of the highest scientific honors any scientist can get in this country, plus an honorary membership in the Franklin Institute. Dr. Kapitza won that award in 1944, for the high quality of his work in atomic science.

The trouble with the secrecy stamp is that it can't keep the Dr. Kapitzas of this planet from their work. It can't keep secret a scientific fact as obvious as the fact that water is wet, that fire is hot, that the sky looks blue. The secrecy stamp did not prevent Dr. Kapitza and his assistants from going to the same source of information as the scientists who had produced our atom bomb—the atom itself. It is the same atom to any scientist, whatever the color of his skin, whatever his politics, whatever language he speaks. Dr. Kapitza worked with the atom to produce a Soviet atomic bomb in exactly the same way as our scientists worked to produce our bomb.

For years before the war, Peter Kapitza had worked and studied at Cambridge, in England. The Royal Society of England, on the recommendation of Lord Ernest Rutherford, gave him two and a half million dollars to set up a nuclear physics laboratory. Lord Rutherford considered Peter Kapitza a prize pupil. Lord Rutherford is considered to be one of the fathers of today's nuclear physics.

Peter Kapitza took that knowledge about nuclear physics back to the U.S.S.R. with him at the end of the 1930s. In training and in knowledge he was and is the equal of any man in the world of atomic science. He is now the head of the Institute for Physical Research in the Soviet Academy of Sciences in Moscow. Dr. Kapitza is part of an international science which is practiced by, and understood by, men of science all over the world. There can be no lasting scientific secrets from such men.

How useless this kind of security effort can be was underscored dramatically by an event that took place in 1945. Graduate students in a physics seminar at the University of

Pennsylvania read about the atomic bomb, and because there was nothing in any physics textbook about this new product of science they decided to write a book about it.

They went to the university library and the library of the Franklin Institute. They hauled off the shelves everything they could find in print on the subject. It was all open material, in magazines, newspapers, books, none of which was restricted or secret. Then they put their heads together, exchanged information, and put out a first draft of the book.

That manuscript brought security agents to the university to find what they thought was a "security leak" that made it possible for those young graduate students to put into writing practically everything about the bomb except the way it was exploded. Those security people could not understand that there are no scientific "secrets" of that kind. The whole idea behind the "secrecy" stamp cannot work in science. There can be no "secret" facts in nature, only a variation in the speed with which men discover the facts. And given the same facilities, the same money and the same encouragement, scientists anywhere in the world can duplicate the work of scientists anywhere else.

As you can read for yourself in the July, 1958, report of the House Special Subcommittee on Government Information, the main reason for our atomic security program in 1945 was to block Soviet science.

Well, the record speaks for itself, although not very loudly because much of that record also is buried under the "secret" stamp. The public has not been given the facts. The facts are that our security program has not exactly been a howling success. The Russians matched our atom bomb in four years. They detonated their first thermonuclear device, a hydrogen blast, less than a year after we did. They made the first step into space with Sputnik, and they put the first man into space.

What this record suggested to the House Subcommittee was that the secret classification of scientific information which began with our 1945 atomic security program lost us our lead in several areas of scientific achievement. By that political decision in 1945, we have not blocked Soviet scientific progress. We have blocked our own scientific progress!

And yet this "secrecy" survives. Each administration has spoken loudly, firmly and long about its intention to close all kinds of gaps, to catch up wherever we're behind. But, our scientists still can't talk freely to other scientists about their work in fields where exchange of information is absolutely vital to progress and leadership in science.

The road we have been traveling, the road of secrecy in science, can be the road to oblivion. If we do not change our course, if our political authorities do not become convinced that there are no secrets that can be concealed for long, and that there is everything to be gained by free exchange of information among the non-communist world's scientists in particular, the possibility is very strong that we will not surpass the Russians.

The idea of exchange has been clouded, too, by extremist views and the efforts of those who favor secrecy. Such persons have indicated that those who do not favor secrecy want our government to open the doors to our arsenals, and let the Russians enter to inspect our techniques of armament making, including H-bombs. Nothing could be further from the truth. The truth is that where it hurts is not in the refusal of our government to give information to the Russians, but in our refusal to let scientists talk over their problems with our allies, the British, the French, the Italians. The position of the security-conscious people is that since there are communists in many of those countries, there will be leaks. Of course, they are absolutely right. There will be some leaks. But, those leaks will be about our advanced scientific accomplishments, a rate of advance not possible to date in security-ridden totalitarian societies, the Soviet Union and its Academy of Sciences notwithstanding. As long as any possible enemy must copy our advanced ideas in science we are not in trouble. There is an important issue at stake in this matter, the issue whether the free society or the totalitarian society is the best way, and the fastest way, to advance to the good life for all men.

The danger of our policy is well illustrated in the development of a proximity fuse, a fuse designed to explode a cannon shell when it comes within the critical area of a target. A gunner need not actually hit the target; so long as the shell comes close, the warhead explodes. Obviously, the proximity fuse is a valuable device.

Several years ago, while this device was still labeled "Top Secret," the Norwegian government got wind of it and sent one of their top scientists here to ask that it be made available to them, as a potential ally, for use in their defense program.

This was impossible, of course. The purpose of our secrecy program was to keep scientific developments like this out of unfriendly hands, and while the Norwegians were anything but unfriendly, still this might slip through them to somebody else.

So home went the Norwegian scientist to work out his own proximity fuse, which he did in less than three years. It was simpler than ours, much more reliable than ours, and cost less. The secret of a proximity fuse could not be kept from a trained scientific mind.

When this happened we sent a team of armament experts over to see that fuse work. The Norwegians showed us their plans, told us whatever we wanted to know. But even then our men could not open their mouths to exchange any information which in this case would have benefited no one but us.

Robert Gross, president of Lockheed Aircraft, told a Congressional committee in Washington that secrecy has made it a matter of years to develop and build a new jet fighter now, whereas before the regulations and restrictions of our secrecy program he could develop and build that kind of plane in about one hundred and ninety days. One of the main reasons for this delay is that Lockheed engineers could not talk about techniques with engineers of other firms brought in as sub-contractors to help build the same plane. Such talk was a violation of existing security regulations, regulations which Albert Einstein said would have made it impossible to build the atomic bomb if they had existed then in science and government. Dr. Einstein spoke with some authority on this subject. No one did more to make the bomb possible, by gathering from all over the world the trained minds needed for the job.

Worst of all, we are hamstringing our own scientists and educators at the very source. Compare the contents of any standard, advanced physics textbook published in this country today with a Soviet textbook or a communist Chinese textbook. Regulations keep vitally important facts and information out of our training books; but not out of theirs. At whom is this "secrecy" weapon aimed anyway?

Secrecy is not the answer to survival. As a matter of fact, it spawns many taboos outside the area of science, affecting our lives in many other ways. It always has, throughout history.

Consider what happened when Galileo Galilei, the Sixteenth Century physicist, broke a taboo. In the world of his day the idea that the earth revolved around the sun was not accepted or approved. Everybody knew the earth was the center of the universe, and that everything moved around it. The moon was not a round world, like ours; it was a hole in a dome that covered a flat earth. The sun had been placed in the sky simply to give man light on earth. These were the facts, the truths of Galileo's world, until Galileo built an astronomical telescope.

Galileo was, in a very real sense, a rebel. Another rebel, James Aitken, was hanged in Eighteenth Century London because he and a few friends tried to burn down the city of London after he had read an incendiary pamphlet by a man who wrote under the name of Poplicola. Since then, that pamphlet has been responsible for quite a bit of history, from the hanging of James Aitken to incidents on street corners in cities and towns all over the United States. One day, a man handing out pamphlets for a locally unpopular political group was ordered off the streets in a city in Southern California by some people who did not like what his group stood for. When the man refused to leave, he was arrested. The complaint was that the ideas printed in the pamphlets he had handed out were "incompatible with social order." Those ideas were dangerous to the community and should not be allowed to get around, the complaint stated.

That case went to the California Supreme Court. Its decision was buried under the story of a U-2 plane that crashed in the U.S.S.R. during a reconnaissance flight over that country for one of our security agencies, a story which had something to do with the defense of our way of life against dangers from outside these United States.

The California Supreme Court, at about the same time, did its share of the work involved in the defense of our way of life against dangers from inside this nation. Its decision amounted to a warning to Americans to learn their history better, if they want a future as a free people.

The gist of the Supreme Court decision was that pamphleteering has deep roots in our history. Roots that go back to *Common Sense* by Thomas Paine, and hundreds of other writings in early America which dealt with ideas that were "incompatible," in fact, downright dangerous to "order." Poplicola, Paine, and their friends spelled out very clearly, in speeches and in writing, a kind of government in which there would always be room for "incompatible" ideas and opinions.

That California Supreme Court decision reiterated one of the most important of all the principles laid down by the founders of the nation.

This nation did not become great and powerful by restricting what people could know and do. These United States today enjoy the good life and world leadership because Americans have enjoyed the greatest freedom to know and do things.

They could and did change conditions as they were in the world when men like Poplicola wrote their "dangerous" ideas back in the 1760s.

The main thing that separates an American of the 1960s from the world of Poplicola's day is our understanding of the part freedom played in our history. Without that understanding, it would not be hard to fall back to things as they were.

Early in 1958, shortly after the U.S.S.R. placed its first Sputnik into space, a meeting was held in Washington to discuss a book that was about to be published, a book which had been authorized several months earlier. Like the judges who tried Galileo over three hundred years earlier, this meeting was to decide how much of certain important facts and truths Americans should be allowed to know. Those people met literally to suppress and distort facts and truth. That meeting was literally an effort to control change. The book involved made it very clear that, if we wanted a future as a free people, the nation would have to overhaul its educational system drastically to meet the challenge of Soviet education that lay behind Sputnik I.

But the meeting succeeeded in suppressing this truth. Many vital facts in the book were left out. The United States Office of Education finally released a version of the book called *Education in the U.S.S.R.* It gave the public, but particularly our government agencies in Washington who desperately needed a book like this, an inaccurate, if not downright false, picture of Soviet education. To this day many of our ideas about what goes on in Soviet classrooms are still affected by what was published then. What was published was not what Eleanor S. Lowman, the book's author, intended. Her services in writing that book had been requested by the Office of Education. She was borrowed from one of our intelligence agencies in Washington to do this job because there was no one in our Office of Education who knew enough about Soviet education to deal with this subject.

What Eleanor Lowman intended was a book that would point up the enormous challenge to our future as a free democracy, and as a leading world power. Her book, as published, presents no such picture.

Why were the facts suppressed?

Because the Office of Education saw Miss Lowman's facts in 1958 in much the same way that a clerical tribunal saw Galileo's facts some three hundred and twenty-five years earlier. Both groups simply refused to believe the accumulating evidence.

In that earlier day, the members of the Inquisition refused even to look through Galileo's telescope to see for themselves the moons of Jupiter, or the mountains of the moon. They simply refused to see the proof of his facts. It was easier then, as it is now, to live with accepted and approved ideas, with comfortable ideas, such as our idea in 1958 that a people like the Russians, under dictatorship, could not possibly do anything worth our concern. It was easier to explain Sputnik I as the work of captured German scientists than to face Miss Lowman's facts that it was the result of a Soviet educational system which was turning out literate people, better educated in specific ways than the products of our schools. The sections of Miss Lowman's original manuscript that pointed this out were cut out of the book by the United States Office of Education. You were not allowed to know the unpleasant truth.

There is no more important thing for Americans to know and to be concerned about. For years nothing did more to keep Americans unconcerned about the challenge of Soviet education and Soviet science than the idea that only in a free democracy could people be really literate and educated. This has long been an accepted and approved idea in the United States, and it is as meaningless an idea as it is a comfortable one.

Youngsters in the schools of a free society are free to waste their time, as well as to make good use of it. As any visitor to the U.S.S.R. who has seen the Soviet schoolroom in action during the past few years can testify, Soviet students lack only the privilege of wasting their time during their school years. This fact may resolve the issue about the free society or the totalitarian society as the best, and the fastest, way to advance to the good life for all men. Time wasted in being spared the truth is a poor investment in this nation's future.

There had been no real American interest in Soviet education before Sputnik I. Eight years before Sputnik I one of our intelligence agencies reported the spectacular rate at which the U.S.S.R. was increasing its supply of scientists and engineers. In 1950 our intelligence agencies began gathering evidence to show that the U.S.S.R. was pouring 10 per cent of its national income into its schools every year, while we were putting about 3 per cent of ours into education. Those reports showed there were more Soviet students majoring in astronomy, astrophysics, geodesy, oceanography, and such specialized subjects, in one single Soviet institution, than there were American students studying these subjects in *all American schools combined.*

That was a decade ago. The proportions have not changed much since then. Whatever visitors of the U.S.S.R. may have to say about the poor workmanship in Russian apartment and office buildings, schools get the best available materials, and they turn out the best possible graduates. Their assumption is that in the Age of Science the future will belong to people who prepare for it.

One would think we might have learned all this from history, because history certainly shows the facts, even back to the days of the Romans.

Early in the Fifth Century, the city of Rome, the heart of the Empire, was in deadly trouble. Rome was surrounded by the Goths; it was about to be invaded. The people were desperate. Never before, in all the history of Rome, was the capital in such danger. In their desperation the Romans turned to some demagogues who told them that the barbarians were at the city gates because of treachery at home. They said that Romans had been sold out by traitors, like Serena, the emperor's adoptive mother. One demagogue held "proof" in his hand before the Roman Senate that Serena had been in secret negotiations with Alaric, the barbarian leader. She was the traitor, he roared.

The crowd listened and approved. What it heard from that man had nothing to do with the truth, as the people were to learn in the days that followed. But they took the demagogue's advice. They put Serena to death, and then the people were astonished to find that this in no way influenced the enemy at the gates. They stayed there, and grew stronger until one day they swarmed in, and the Roman Empire went the way of all civilizations that were inherited by people who preferred comfortable, accepted and approved ideas to change; people who preferred scapegoats to facts.

The facts behind those final days of Rome were that Romans refused to believe the evidence, accumulating for years, that the Goths had been developing their armed strength, using tactics and techniques the Romans had used before them. This is an old historical pattern. It has been going on for a long time, and it is going on right now, in our time.

Another fact about those final days of Rome was that the smug and comfortable Romans of the Fifth Century A.D. were not the Romans of the Second Century B.C. who built the Empire. The people of the Empire enjoyed what the Republic had made possible, without understanding history; without understanding what made their Empire possible. They underestimated their competitors.

It was much easier to live with the old idea that the barbarian Goths, with their lower standard of living, could not possibly do anything worth Roman concern. It was easier to explain falling prestige and lagging military power by hunting out supposed subversives and traitors like Serena, than it was to face the fact that in Fifth Century Rome the emptiest places in the city were the libraries. The fullest places were the circuses where Romans screamed themselves hoarse betting on the chariot races. Roman schoolrooms educated the young to the pleasure of ease and luxury. It was an education hardly suited to match the vigor and strength of the invaders.

Adult Romans, you see, preferred not to be disturbed.

Does all this sound familiar? Well, it is written in Gibbon's *Decline and Fall of the Roman Empire*. If it sounds familiar, it should. Change a few dates, a few names, a few places, and you could come very close to our time, as close as a man named Lawrence Johnson, a grocer in Syracuse, New York, and as close as a fellow named Poplicola, a writer who lived in Eighteenth Century Boston, Massachusetts.

Poplicola's ideas extended across an ocean to so inflame James Aitken that he acted on them and was hanged. Poplicola and his friends worked out the cornerstone of a unique kind of government. They had a strange idea for their time. It was that every man and woman had a God-given free will, and a God-given responsibility to use it to govern himself, and to make lives of dignity possible for all men. Men and women could not use that free will responsibly as long as they accepted unquestioningly the order of things generally approved. It was the obligation of all free men to question everything, those men said, in order to know. It was the obligation of all free men to disagree with evil, to dissent against ignorance, against bigotry, and poverty, and greed, and stupidity. *Dissent,* these men said—and *improve* things.

Poplicola and his friends built these ideas into a form of government which they hoped would make it possible for free men to use their free wills to work out problems.

Two hundred years after Poplicola (the nom de plume of the American patriot Samuel Adams), Lawrence Johnson, a grocer in Syracuse, New York, made that program work. He made it work so effectively that the television industry still hasn't completely recovered from his influence on what Americans have seen on their TV screens since 1952. It is a fascinating story about what one determined and dedicated man can do in a free society.

Mr. Johnson literally terrorized the television industry. Every time Mr. Johnson heard a program he did not like he sat down and wrote the network that carried it, the agency that handled it, and the sponsor who paid for it. He stated his views about any and all provocative or controversial programs. He did not like them. He wanted them off the air.

Mr. Johnson, ironically, did not recognize the right of individual Americans to question anything or to dissent from anything.

Now, the point is not whether Mr. Johnson was right or wrong in his views about the programs. His right to express his views to networks, agencies, and sponsors is not in question either.

What is important is that because of frightened men in television's high places during the middle fifties, and because of the ignorance and apathy of great numbers of Americans about how we work as a political democracy, Mr. Johnson, almost single-handedly, pushed controversial programs off the air.

Today the air is full of bland, gutless, irrelevant programs. Why? Because too many Americans could not match Lawrence Johnson's sustained, continuing faith in the way we work as a democracy. The point is that Mr. Johnson acted. He acted on what he believed. He showed what the power of the individual, exercising a free will, can do in a free soceity.

The point is also that this way of life of ours has no *guarantee* of freedom; only the possibility. It can be used in two ways, either by men like the Lawrence Johnsons who favor the taboos, or by those who favor freedom.

So here are two more key challenges to freedom, taboos and censorship. They are really different faces of the same challenge, the right of every American to know, and the responsibility of every American to make it possible for his children to learn.

Ignorance is not bliss in the Age of Science. It was a dangerous kind of ignorance of science that made "secrecy" possible in the first place. There are no gentle words to describe that kind of security or taboo. Not any more. They are deadly to the future of this nation. We are behind in certain critical scientific areas just as the 1958 report of the House Special Subcommittee on Information pointed out. This is the case because we have failed to follow two very important, very basic American principles: freedom and competition.

This nation, as was pointed out in Chapter Two, once believed that there was nothing like competition between ideas in a free land to produce the best thinkers: the best Fords, Edisons and Einsteins. We became a great nation in large part because of that belief. We were secure yesterday because of what those minds enabled us to do. We were secure because of what we achieved. All that has changed. Now we are a nation belabored by rubber stamps marked "secret." There is no security in hiding, or in concealment. There never has been.

Despite this, we remain the same nation, and the same principles and beliefs that made us great are still available to us, waiting for the people—that is, for us—to demand that they be respected again.

CHAPTER 8

Science and Survival

IN AUGUST, 1940, an ordinary suitcase was flown across the Atlantic Ocean from London to Washington. Its appearance was ordinary but its contents were not. In it was the most valuable cargo ever transported to the United States. Its contents spelled victory in World War II.

Among its contents were plans for the construction of an instrument called the magnetron. It was a particular kind of magnetron invented in England in 1940, and it became the most important single scientific development for the Allies in World War II. It led directly to the perfection of radar, the weapon which made it possible for Great Britain to survive the Battle of Britain in 1940.

Around that electronic device the British built their air defense. Specially trained squadrons of fighter planes intercepted German bombers whenever they were spotted on that early radar screen. The magnetron, and the radar that was developed from it, gave us the time we needed to prepare for our part in World War II. In the Pacific, during the year following Pearl Harbor, radar allowed our weakened naval forces to hold off what was then a superior Japanese sea power.

The magnetron saved our future, but it put an end to an important part of our past. It was part of the new basis of power in the world that evolved out of World War II. The power of science. That power is the key to the future in ways that are not yet clear to many Americans.

For example, not many Americans were particularly impressed by a news item that appeared in the press in March, 1961, which told about the results of a scientific experiment that took place in the laboratories of the Boeing Aircraft Company of Seattle, Washington. Large, transparent containers with single-celled plants called algae were attached to an airtight tank. A man walked into that tank and was sealed off from any contact with air outside the tank for fifty-seven hours. He came out alive. Normally, anyone sealed into an air-tight air space 9 x 15 feet in size would not stay alive very long. This was not a normal air space, because it was attached to those banks of tubes—filled with algae.

As soon as the man entered that tank, powerful lights were focused on the tubes, and those single-celled plants began working over the air in that tank to keep it breathable, to keep that man alive as he, or any future astronaut or space traveler, would have to be kept alive on long trips to other planets, or to the stars. As the man breathed out carbon dioxide the algae absorbed it and used it to turn out oxygen.

This was an experiment to develop what is known as a "life-support" system. For fifty-seven hours, those plants supported a human life in that tank because of the green miracle in the plants, the chlorophyll, which (for reasons scientists still do not understand completely) takes energy out of light in the process of photosynthesis. Using the energy from light, plants give off oxygen while producing the carbohydrates, fats, and proteins space travelers will need. And both these items, air and food, are in one package, instead of the tons of containers of canned air and canned food that would have to be hauled around the universe to keep tomorrow's space travelers alive.

That experiment in the Boeing aircraft laboratory was vital to us. So are others like it now being conducted around the nation. They can be the key to man's future in space.

But this fact was not understood in some of the highest places only a few years ago when the nation learned that, in fields such as rocketry and space research, Soviet science was moving ahead of ours. At that time, a member of the Cabinet of the United States told the nation that he wasn't particularly concerned about the situation; that he was more concerned abou cutting back spending by his department. He was not interested, he said, in research that would not produce what he described as "useful" or "valuable" results.

He meant, for example, to eliminate work then under way by the Navy to find out why grass is green. It was an important subject, but practically all the people who make decisions about such scientific matters, like that Cabinet member, did not know this. Which brings us face to face with a little-understood but very serious problem. The problem is an important difference between the President of the United States and his Cabinet on the one hand, and on the other hand the Premier of the U.S.S.R. and his Presidium, the ruling group of men around Mr. Khrushchev. Not one of the nation's top men sitting as the Cabinet of the United States during Mr. Kennedy's first year in office was fitted, by training or by background, to deal at first hand with the facts of power changed through science in our time; facts like, why grass is green.

Men with nonscientific backgrounds simply do not see the kind of world that the fifteen members of the Soviet Presidium see. Nine of those fifteen top men sitting in those high Soviet places were trained as scientists or engineers. They have been dealing at first hand with the changing facts of power through science, making the top level decisions which have moved Soviet science and research ahead of ours in rocketry and space programs. They have made decisions which have placed a third of mankind and a third of the world's real estate under communist control.

This is no criticism of lawyers, bankers, business executives, economists, and the variety of social scientists who, with a few exceptions, have composed the cabinets of every American administration through the past twenty years. But during those years the facts of power and the basis of power have altered.

So serious problems begin with this difference between the two groups of men: What they recognize as the facts of power today and what they do about those facts.

There is a second part of this problem which concerns a fellow I shall call Joe Smith and something Joe Smith did. Not long ago he made Mr. Khrushchev and his friends more confident than ever that the world will indeed be a communist one in our time.

Mr. Smith is not a communist. He is an inventor who lives in a fairly large city in the western United States. About three years ago, Joe Smith stumbled onto a new idea for an engine to power automobiles and airplanes better than ever before. This engine could be used to power rockets through space, too.

Joe Smith worked out his idea carefully and then went through the same experience most American inventors have known. He could not get the right people interested in using his idea. In the first place, he was told, it would not work. It did not fit any kind of motor power that was known.

He was told this by the same type of people who had solemnly assured the Wright brothers that their flying machine would not work either. Company after company turned Joe down. Government agencies were not interested because Joe Smith's idea did not guarantee any useful, practical results.

Three years of frustration left Joe Smith disappointed and

broke. Then he remembered something he had heard at a science convention about scientific societies in Europe that were looking for basic ideas turned out by the Joe Smiths of the world. Those societies paid well for some ideas, too.

After checking, Joe Smith sent a letter outlining his new idea to a society in Western Europe. He received an immediate reply from that scientific society telling him that his idea interested them very much. If, after study by their experts, it proved to be a workable idea, they were prepared to pay him a very sizable chunk of cash, in American dollars.

After study by their experts, it did prove to be a workable idea, and Mr. Smith was, soon afterward, still a frustrated American inventor, but no longer broke. He was paid very well for an idea which was studied very carefully by experts located at 14 Leninski Lane, Moscow, U.S.S.R.

The scientific organization in Western Europe to which Joe Smith wrote was a foreign agency, one of many combing the world for ideas to strengthen the Soviet Academy of Sciences. Joe Smith's scientific idea landed in Moscow because there they have an awareness of the value of his kind of science.

Until the time that fateful suitcase carried its valuable cargo into the United States in 1940, we Americans never had to worry about that kind of science. Afterward, however, we had good reason to worry about it, a reason that concerns a young man by the name of Peter Starovsky.

In August, 1960, we were testing a rocket plane, the X-15, in flight. On that occasion it went twenty-five miles up, and traveled at a speed of nearly three thousand miles an hour. This was one of the ways we have been working to put a manned probe into space, and as we worked, our program was being studied with great care by a Soviet physics student whom I met at that time in the Lenin Library in Moscow.

The Lenin Library is a repository library, much like the Library of Congress, where publications from all places on earth are kept on file. I met Peter Starovsky in the section set aside for aeronautics and space publications. He was sitting at a table piled high with books and magazines from the United States which mentioned the work being done to develop the X-15 into a manned space probe.

Peter was a fourth-year student at the University of Moscow, and the X-15 was a special assignment in his main field of study, the field of propulsion. As he explained it to me, his assignment was to study the propulsion system of our rocket plane. Then he was to work out a theoretical substitute for that propulsion system, some kind of drive that would do the same job better.

Now what this means is Peter was being trained by the Soviet Union in both theoretical and applied physics in the hope that he might work out a completely new idea about how to move things. In other words, he was to do what Joe Smith, American inventor, had done. Unlike Joe Smith, however, Peter would have no trouble getting his idea developed.

Obviously, the word "science" does not mean the same thing in the U.S. and the U.S.S.R.

An American manufacturer of a hair-fixing preparation for American women announced recently that his product was the "greatest scientific advance in years," the product of years of research. Several years ago, one of our leading cigarette companies informed the public about the "revolutionary" results of "scientific research" in its laboratories carried out by many "highly trained scientists and technicians" who had strained their minds to put a new top on a cigarette package.

Obviously, Americans see science as a way to turn out more and better ballpoint pens and refrigerators; and hairpins with more kinks in them than ever before; more and better consumer goods to live the good life with.

The communist countries do not use their science or research for this purpose. They use our science and our research to give their people hair sprays, flip-top boxes and hairpins, simply by copying these things. For example, Soviet-made cameras are now on sale in this country. Any camera fan will see at once that they look just like outstanding German or Swedish or Japanese models. They should resemble them; they are almost exact copies.

Throughout Asia, you can find Chinese communist cigarette lighters, copied exactly from Austrian originals; Chinese bicycles, that look just like their British originals. By letting other people research and develop better consumer goods, then copying them, the communist countries save their money and effort for more important scientific research.

They save their energies for the research that will produce new propulsion systems, new kinds of energy to change the basis of power in the world, just as the idea that all matter is energy changed the world through the development of atomic energy. Since World War II, when the communist countries talk about science and research, they mean they are pouring their energies into working from basic theoretical ideas toward technological revolutions which they can direct to produce a communist future for the human race.

Because of this revolution in science, Peter Starovsky is a very important man in our future, and a serious threat because of what he will be trained to do by the time he finishes his five and a half year program for his university degree in theoretical physics. What he has been trained to do has put an end to our past, the kind that lasted until that suitcase reached this country in August, 1940. Behind that suitcase is an important kind of history few Americans know.

It is the kind of history that made it possible for an American named Edison to invent an electric light. First, men named Maxwell, Faraday, Hertz, and Thomson produced theories about electricity. Edison then used their theories to make his light. Becquerel theorized his way into basic ideas about radioactivity, which were much later transformed in this country into atomic energy. Sir Arthur Fleming theorized his way to penicillin, one of the most important basic ideas in medical science today.

We took the ideas of those men, who were not American scientists, but were theoretical scientists doing basic research someplace else, and we applied their ideas to electric lights, television sets, jet engines, and nuclear reactors. We did that until the World War II suitcase incident. That suitcase carried one of the last shipments of other people's basic ideas to this country. World War II and the cold war have cut off that supply of ideas from other places for the first time in our history.

All of which poses an important question: where are the ideas to come from in the future? American schools have not turned out many theoretical scientists in the past; and, for the most part, they are not turning them out today. Most of the laboratories in which most of our scientifically trained people work are not studying basic research, problems such as why grass is green, to make plants the basis for "life support" systems in our race to space, or new propulsion systems. We have never been particularly interested in such things, although out of this theoretical work have come all of the things that made us a great industrial nation.

Do the nation's lawyers, businessmen, economists, bankers, and the rest, in government or out of it, have an answer to this problem? Do they know the problem exists? Do they know why Peter Starovsky is a double threat to their future? Not if you read the views expressed in 1961 by a man who heads one of the nation's largest industries. He wrote an article in one of our national magazines stating that he was fed up with our overriding concern about what the communist nations are doing in science and technology. We are spending too much time and effort trying to match the U.S.S.R.'s accomplishments in such things as space research, and there is no need to do this, this businessman said.

Instead we should do what we consider to be important in

terms of our own scientific needs. Let the Soviet Union wear itself out in leading the race to space. Let America do what Americans do best in science. This brought us the world's highest living standards in the past, and it benefited the whole world, too.

It is a powerful complaint by a leading American who misunderstands the kind of world he lives in. He also misreads history. No nation, no people, at any time in history, have been able to survive by following that kind of program. No nation, no people have ever been able to live out their lives on their own terms.

If that important business leader were advised to run his business as he suggests the nation run its foreign affairs, he would consider such a suggestion ill-advised, and that's a polite word for it. Suppose his company were to discover suddenly that one of its competitors had found a way to produce things at half the price that his company has to charge, challenging his company's markets, taking away his customers. Suppose, too, this competitor claimed that his way of doing business was much better, that all future investors should invest in that company.

Given this economic situation, in simple business terms, how long do you suppose that businessman would go on doing business in the same old way, doing what he did best, and ignoring his competition? That situation is not one whit different from the political competition that now exists between America and the West on the one side, and the communist powers on the other. In both instances, you can ignore your competition only at your own great peril.

There is nothing wrong with this nation, scientifically or otherwise, that could not be cured by a strong dose of personal responsibility. Responsibility is needed to recognize that power will be achieved and held through science in our time.

The communist countries see science as their most important weapon; a tool to use in controlling the future of the world.

We seemed to understand this well enough when our survival as a nation was at stake during World War II. At that time, we set up the wartime Office of Scientific Research and Development. Although that office was geared for war, most of the consumer goods that we take as the measure of the good life today came out of its basic research projects.

The nation's survival is at stake again today, and we need a Secretary of Scientific Research and Development with full Cabinet status to meet our problems of survival. It is not enough to have scientific advisors to the politicians. You must put science on the same level with the politicians, if the arguments of science are to be heard.

It is also the responsibility of men and women in high places, and in low places as well, to recognize that the future is being decided right now on top government levels and in the classrooms of two countries—the United States and the U.S.S.R.

Out of the Soviet Union's classrooms came Peter Starovsky. What is happening now in the classrooms of our communities to prepare tomorrow's Americans to meet the challenge posed by Peter Starovsky?

As throughout history, the future still belongs to those who have prepared for it best.

CHAPTER 9

Resources for Survival

LASHIO, BURMA, is a long way from Rock Island, Illinois. Very few Rock Islanders had ever heard of the place. Tokyo, Japan, is not quite as far from that Burmese place, but it would be safe to say that very few people in Japan's capital city had ever heard of it either. However, there were people in both places who did know about what was happening in and around Lashio during the winter of 1938. In both places, they were most concerned about Lashio.

In both places, a few Americans and Japanese were concerned about wolframite, scheelite and tungstite. Lashio was a transfer point for trucks and caravans moving those minerals, among other things, out of China on the Burma Road. Twenty years after one hundred sixty thousand Chinese literally hacked and clawed their way across the foothills of the Himalayan Mountains, to build that road and open a "back door" into China, it was possible to read through a number of American

125

history books without finding a single reference to the Burma Road, or to those minerals. This is more than a little strange, in view of the fact that history turned for us on that road. Soon after the Burma Road opened, because of those minerals, the world turned into a kind of place that most Americans do not recognize even now.

The several people in Rock Island, Illinois, who knew about Lashio at that time were design engineers at the military arsenal in that city. Early in 1938, they received an important assignment from Washington. It was two years after the Spanish Civil War, which had been a kind of military proving ground for the armies of Italy, Germany, Russia, Britain and France. Most Americans did not know it, but American weapons got into that Spanish war, too. The reports that came from the battlefields of Spain made it quite clear that we would have to bring our military hardware up to date. The Germans, under the Nazis, had made great advances in weapons, and no nation could afford to lag behind.

So to the Rock Island Arsenal came an order: develop an armor-piercing shell, one that could be used against motorized, armored divisions, the kind American troops were to face in a few very short years on every battlefield from Normandy to Iwo Jima.

The design engineers at Rock Island were worried about this assignment, not because they lacked ideas, but because they needed a special kind of metal to do the job. Such metal could be made, but in 1938 the necessary ingredients were in short supply. What those men needed was a heavy carbide of the metal made from wolframite, scheelite and tungstite. The metal? Tungsten.

As the *Minerals Yearbook* for the years immediately preceding World War II points out, America then imported half the tungsten ore used in this country. Our main source of supply was China. But the Japanese had moved into China in 1931. By 1938, the Japanese controlled the supply of these minerals by controlling the roads and rivers of China. One of Imperial Japan's main goals in China, as it was soon to be for all Asia, was to control such resources and keep them out of the hands of possible enemies. One "possible enemy" was the United States.

For this reason, Japan's military planners in Tokyo were concerned about what was happening in and around Lashio in the winter of 1938. They knew what wolframite and the rest of those resources meant to the design engineers in Rock Island, Illinois.

History turned for the Japanese, too, on that Burma Road. In the few years before World War II spread to Asia, the tungsten that reached us by way of Lashio gave America the time to find other sources to turn out millions of armor-penetrating shells. These were indeed "resources of survival."

Most Americans then did not understand the problems of resources and survival, largely because this is not the kind of history we get in our history or economics books. Most Americans, to this day, do not understand the kind of world we entered in the late 1930s and early 1940s on the Burma Road.

When the Japanese attacked Burma in May, 1942, they headed straight for the Burma Road. We were informed at the time that they did so because they were worried about the arms and supplies America was sending east on that road to China's armies. That was not the whole story. The Japanese moved swiftly to close the Burma Road because they were worried about what was being carried west on that road, to make the tools and machinery of war in American factories.

In a remarkably efficient military campaign, Imperial Japanese troops moved inland, cutting through heavy forests and impossibly rough terrain, laying down roads and railroads as supply lines, to reach and cut that Burma Road in less than six months.

They arrived too late. By May, 1942, America's own production of tungsten metals was rolling. We were beginning to receive these "resources of survival" from other places. But history could have been very different for us if the Japanese had cut the Burma Road earlier; if that miracle road which ended at Lashio had not been opened on Christmas Day, 1938.

This tale is not just history. The resources for survival are more important than ever, as the Soviet Union's military high command knows, with its heavy emphasis on the submarine, the backbone of its offensive power on the seas.

The U.S.S.R. has at least five hundred submarines today, several of them known to be nuclear-powered. The Soviets today have the largest undersea fleet in the world. Since the end of World War II the Soviet Union has concentrated on building this type of warship, rather than trying to match the western powers in destroyers, cruisers, and aircraft carriers.

This is a point that has mystified John Q. American. He does not see submarines as the backbone of a modern navy. He was not particularly impressed by Mr. Khrushchev's statement a few years ago that surface navies and air power were obsolete.

The Soviet leader announced at that time that his country was scrapping plans for such obsolete weapons. The Soviet Union's military planners were following a different line, a different strategy.

Neither was John Q. particularly concerned when he read that Soviet submarines, and fishing trawlers, have been sighted along the main shipping lanes, and at various places off the coasts of North and South America from time to time. Some of the news reports he has read and heard about these "fishing" boats say they're loaded with electronic equipment for tracking our missiles, for oceanographic soundings, and for mapping the sea floor.

This is disturbing news, but our government has an answer to this "different strategy" that Mr. Khrushchev mentioned. A short time ago America launched its first nuclear-powered aircraft carrier, part of our Atomic Age navy. Now, this is understandable power, anywhere. This atomic ship, and its air power, can move anywhere on earth to back up our goals in war or in peace. As long as factories and shipyards can turn out jet planes and that aircraft carrier, our security is assured.

About all that John Q. American is absolutely right. As long as American factories and shipyards keep turning out instruments of war and of peace, we will be strong, prosperous, and secure. Mr. Khrushchev and the world's communist leaders know this as well as John Q. American does. But they know something else that John Q. does not know.

Without the minerals baddeleyite and pentlandite, and arsenical ore, and particularly certain laterite material, American factories and shipyards would be hard put to turn out nuclear power plants for our Atomic Age navy, or those jet planes which spell our security.

From baddeleyite comes zirconium, the base for refractories used in the combustion chambers of jet engines, and as construction material for atomic reactors. Where does it come from? From Canada, Brazil, India, Australia, Africa, Japan, and Korea, among other places.

That apparently unimportant news item, discussed in Chapter One, about the American nickel plant in Louisiana which lay idle after the Cuban revolution, is a measure of the danger to our lives in the "different strategy" of Mr. Khrushchev.

When America was unable to get nickel ore from Cuba, our government turned to other places. In the case of cobalt, we got much of our supply from Katanga in the Belgian Congo. By a very interesting coincidence, communist activity increased in the Congo. Katanga became a center of revolution, just as Cuba did. *Is* it a coincidence?

Without nickel and cobalt our defenses would suffer. This was the reason for the stockpiling program that came under Congressional scrutiny in February, 1962. Those stockpiles reflected imports to meet our shortages, or lack of critical materials in the event of war. There would be far less security for Americans without those materials. There would be fewer top quality engines for our Strategic Air Command; less powerful rocket engines to support our space program. Materials like nickel and cobalt are vital in the production of the highest heat-resistant metals for such engines. Because nickel happens to be one of forty-eight different materials we import to make our telephones; and one of the thirty-eight materials we import to make our automobiles; and because it goes into our television sets, our radios, our electric toasters and many other things, there would be much less of the good life for us without it.

The point is that in today's world, as never before in history, whoever controls the world's mineral resources can control the world. That point becomes significant in light of the fact that none of the western powers has, inside its own territories, the minerals and metals it needs to be strong in war or peace.

Remember Suez, and what cutting off just one important raw material, oil, did to every European economy? That can be repeated indefinitely by means short of war, such as political and economic influence in the affairs of the countries exporting raw materials. If a hot war should be necessary to do this, what better way to keep raw materials from the western world's factories than a large, efficient submarine fleet to sink ships?

This is one of the most vital but poorly understood long-range goals of the Soviet Union and communist China.

One of the most important matters discussed in the 1960 presidential campaign was "economic growth." John Kennedy and Richard Nixon both talked about economic growth. They discussed how fast our economy ought to grow in the future. But neither Mr. Kennedy nor Mr. Nixon, nor their economic advisors, showed any doubt that this was the main economic issue facing the nation. Their concern was, how fast do we *want* to grow in the future.

Well, there is another side to that question; another way of thinking about it. How fast *can* we grow in the future?

In 1939 our demand for goods made from strategic materials exceeded our home supply of those materials. We did not have enough of those minerals and metals, of the right kind or quality, to support us in the manner to which we were accustomed then, or are accustomed now.

Until 1939 our economy could expand on our own resources. In 1939 we imported about a dozen so-called strategic materials. Read what your *Minerals Yearbook* has to say about what we have been importing since then to keep our economy growing.

What do you suppose will happen to our future economic growth if other American factories are faced with the same problem as that nickel-cobalt plant in Louisiana?

Today we import more than seventy strategic materials to meet the needs of American factories. Does our economy grow just because we want it to? Or does our economy, like any other economy, grow within the limits set by the availability of resources?

CHAPTER 10

The Atom and the Equalizer

IN 1954, SCIENTISTS in one of the Soviet Union's atomic energy laboratories created a nightmare for us. It grew out of an experiment using a special kind of centrifuge, a device used to whirl chemical compounds at high speed and separate their elements.

That day, although it was not to be known generally for six years, the Soviet scientists whirled a bit of our world out of existence. They separated the gases of different uranium isotopes, by weight, and produced uranium 235 more cheaply and more easily than it had ever before been produced.

To the man on the street anywhere in the world that was just another scientific fact, interesting if you were interested in scientific facts. But, in the language of power, that gaseous centrifuge was as much a symbol of the power to control as was the Colt .44, when it changed the course of history on the American frontier a century ago.

With a .44 in hand, the weakest runt of the American frontier could stand up to the strongest man. That revolver equalized power among men. It was called "the equalizer," for the same reason that the gaseous centrifuge in that Soviet laboratory can be called the equalizer now.

That centrifuge can be the revolution, the nightmare, of the world in ten, or perhaps fifteen years because it can equalize destructive power among men. Consider the significance of that statement as it could be involved in some revolution, somewhere, in the future. Visualize a revolution under way in some South American country, for example. The rebels will have weapons that include missiles, short-range and long-range, with atomic warheads. How will those revolutionists get atomic warheads? They will buy them, just as revolutionists have bought rifles and cannons in the past. In tomorrow's world, with uranium 235 produced easily and cheaply, atomic warheads will take their place in armament sales, along with rifles and cannon. At least thirty countries will have the facilities to produce atomic bombs.

At some point in that future revolution, somewhere south of our borders, the leader of those rebel forces decides to try for a quick knockout blow against his enemies. He decides to use his missiles and atom bombs. In a matter of minutes, the capital city is a pile of radioactive rubble.

During this attack, the government forces will not twiddle their military thumbs. After or during rebel attack, the government sends off a few missiles with warheads of its own; missiles it bought from, or was given by, a friendly bigger power, as part of that power's foreign policy. That atomic reply nearly wipes out the rebel army. Furious and desperate, as losers in war can be, the few revolutionists left alive blame that bigger power for their defeat; and they show how they feel about that by firing off their remaining missiles at the big power's main cities.

Does that sound like a fantastic dream? It isn't. It is entirely possible.

The first step toward such a future event was taken early in 1960, by an industrial firm named the Degussa Company in West Germany. Degussa produced, for sale on world markets, an improved version of that gaseous centrifuge originally built in the U.S.S.R. Brazil promptly bought two of them. A number of other countries put in requests, too: Egypt, Cuba, and communist China.

At least three billion dollars went into the gaseous diffusion plants Americans built to turn out uranium 235; to power our nuclear reactors and explode our atom bombs. And that outlay of money does not include the cost of all that goes with those diffusion plants in installations like Oak Ridge, Los Alamos and the Hanford atomic energy plants. To run those three diffusion plants we used a full 10 per cent of this nation's entire output of electricity—more electrical power than exists in most countries. In this fact, that uranium fuel was expensive, there was a measure of safety for the wealthy and powerful nations, the atomic powers and world leaders.

For those nations, the United States, the Soviet Union, and Great Britain, and more recently, France, that safety is now gone. That old world does not exist any more, and one of the reasons it does not exist is the gaseous centrifuge, which moved from an atomic energy laboratory in the U.S.S.R. in 1954 to world markets through a West German company in 1960. The centrifuge costs only a fraction of the billions we spent on atomic power, and it requires only one-tenth as much electricity to do the same job. To the great nations who had the power to rule the world's political and economic roosts only yesterday, that relatively cheap gaseous centrifuge can mean a new balance of power.

History is repeating itself, changing the political and economic rules of our time for the same old, basic and simple reasons. The centrifuge can be an equalizer, like the Colt revolver.

The Colt took power out of the hands of the few, and put it into the hands of the many.

Unfortunately there is very little evidence to show that either the leaders or the people in the big nations see this change. In hundreds of meetings in Geneva, the three big powers have conferred about a treaty to govern nuclear weapons tests. The approach to these conferences follows some very questionable, outdated rules. Since 1958, the first three countries to become atomic powers have been balancing this power against each other in the old, familiar game of power politics. They seem to assume that atomic power is just another kind of power; that Russia, Great Britain, and America can speak for the whole world in working out ways to control the uses of atomic energy.

Here we tread on dangerous ground. Atomic power is not just another kind of power. The power politics of gunpowder, coal, and oil are obsolete in the Atomic Age; as obsolete as the power politics of the Stone Age became in the Iron Age. The idea that those three powers in Geneva can speak for the world in deciding how the power in the atom will be used in the future is completely out of date.

The French pointed out these facts in 1959, shortly before they exploded their first atomic bomb to become the world's fourth atomic power. To meet the costs of producing the atom bomb, France was reportedly ready to sell atomic weapons to its friends, friends like the Swiss. What the French did in February, 1960, to become an atomic power, communist China will do very soon. China has atomic reactors, too, provided by the Russians, and that country has much the same kind of equipment the French used to build their first bomb. So do at least eight other countries. Once the explosive atomic material is available, the uranium or plutonium, there is no secret about making the bomb.

What, then, is there to prevent China, or any of the other eight countries, from following the French example? They will sell or give atomic weapons to their friends, friends like that future rebel leader, for that future revolution that will be fought with atomic weapons.

There is nothing to prevent it. The three big powers have set up no blueprint of controls over atomic weapons. There are no binding treaties, no international laws, no international agreements to cover atomic energy. The Big Three nations no longer have the power to decide these matters. The big nations are not dealing with the realities of the world.

As of February, 1961, there was only one American factory actually producing long-range missiles. It is not doing so now, but if it were necessary, that one plant could turn out ICBM missiles at a rate of about one a day, or three hundred a year. We could, in an emergency, raise that figure to around twelve hundred missiles a year, by using other facilities.

These facts are known to Russia, our main competitor among the nations of the world. Russia has been in the business of turning out missiles even longer than we have. The U.S.S.R.'s output of missiles each year is not a matter of public information; but it would be safe to assume that their missile plants at least match America's output.

It is important to keep that in mind when playing the game some of our top military experts and academic brains have been playing since the end of World War II.

That game has literally produced tons of printed material dealing with the strategy of war in the Atomic Age. Some titles have to do with limited wars; others refer to wars with conventional weapons, with nuclear weapons, chemical warfare, bacteriological warfare. Based on all this is an equally impressive pile of printed pages concerned with defense against such war.

Since the Federal Civil Defense Administration was set up by President Truman in 1949, more than a billion dollars has gone into the planning of civil defense, with results that range from bomb shelters in basements to plans for the evacuation of whole populations out of our cities and towns.

One pamphlet tells how to stock a bomb shelter in order to survive an H-bomb attack in a typical American city. Properly equipped, it says, a varying number of people could survive the necessary two-week period after a nuclear attack. That is the estimated time required for radioactive fallout on the ground to become harmless. They could then come out, start rebuilding, and do whatever would be needed to carry on a war.

The plan is laid out simply and logically, to meet the kind of war our military planners have been writing about. Unfortunately, it does not have much to do with the reality of atomic war *against which there is no defense.*

At this instant there is no more important reality in the world than this fact. There is no defense in this kind of war, as anyone given the facts about the effects of an H-bomb blast could understand.

One of the most important of those facts was stated plainly a few years ago in a book called *Tomorrow,* written by Philip Wylie. Mr. Wylie was appointed in 1949, by President Truman, as consultant for the Federal Civil Defense Administration. Wylie described a "firestorm," a whole city set aflame by the massive heat of an H-bomb blast. Imagine setting fire to every burnable object in a three-hundred-square-mile area: wooden houses, broken gas mains, gasoline storage tanks. Anyone in any kind of shelter under that kind of city-wide fire would be roasted alive or suffocated.

Nor is this a wild speculation. Proof that this will happen came in the firestorm that followed the World War II bombing of Hamburg, Germany. So many small fires were started in one day by a huge air raid that they merged into a single mass of flames. Few Germans in that city were left alive to talk about it.

Civil defense hopes for survival in the Atomic Age are not based on the reality of war today, but on war as envisioned by university professors and military men who have tried hard to cram a new form of power into an old, familiar framework.

It was not too many years back that military men tried this same routine with air power, preferring the old and the familiar to General Billy Mitchell's view of things to come. They were as wrong then as they are now.

There is nothing to support the idea that a potential aggressor would limit himself to one H-bomb per city. What happens to those properly stocked bomb shelters if, with hundreds of missiles on hand, an aggressor decides to stagger his attacks, sending an H-bomb every other day, or every other week, into one area? What kind of shelter could keep anyone alive for months?

Out of simple curiosity I decided to check into the cost for a properly stocked, air-and-water-filtered shelter able to support human life for one or two months. I gave up when the cost of the necessary equipment went over sixteen thousand dollars for a family of five.

The purpose in making this statement is not to frighten anyone with "scare" facts, but to make clear the realities in today's world; the changing rules of war and peace. The new rules do not fit the old thinking about war or defense.

The first reality is that there is *no defense* against the power of the atom.

The second reality is that the most vulnerable nations in atomic war are the industrial nations; not Egypt, Cuba, or communist China.

The third reality is that more is involved in today's kind of war than a portion of a population: the very future of industrial civilization hangs in the atomic balance.

The atom has begun to equalize the differences between nations in their power to make war. It can also remove some of the more important differences between nations that have led to war in the past.

For example, take two kinds of iron ore: ore from the Mesabi mountains of Minnesota, and ordinary granite, which is widely spread around the earth's surface. Granite is not normally considered to be an iron ore, largely because of the amount of energy that is needed to extract a worthwhile amount of iron from it. About 60 per cent of the Mesabi iron ore is iron. Only about 5 per cent of granite is iron. It is too expensive to use the power necessary to get so little iron out of granite.

But make great quantities of power available cheaply, and that picture changes. The power in the atom can take iron ore from granite, and there is much more granite in the world than there is rich Mesabi ore in Minnesota.

The power in the atom can transform useless land from barren, lifeless desert into productive farmland. The only major difference is water. That is all it takes to make most of the world's dry lands fertile. Three-quarters of the earth's surface is covered with water. The main stumbling block that prevents using ocean water for this purpose today is the amount of energy that has been needed to extract the salt. But, make great quantities of power available, cheaply, and this picture changes. The power in the atom can desalt ocean water. It can make fruitful the 20 per cent of the land mass of this planet which is now barren.

Such things are possible. More than that, this must be done. We have not thought about using the power in the atom that way. Our leaders have not put as much effort into working out a strategy of peace, as has gone into working out a strategy of war. We need a strategy of peace, to accomplish what no strategy of war can, to make sure that there will be a future for our industrial way of life.

The greatest threat to that future concerns the two examples mentioned. The need for metals and food to meet the growing demands of an exploding population around the world.

More and more people are born daily into parts of the world where there are not enough resources to feed them, house them, or clothe them. Increasing numbers of children will grow into increasingly dissatisfied adults in this world where economic development is not keeping up with population, and where the atomic power to destroy is becoming so readily and cheaply available.

That was not what the Hans Bethes, the Albert Einsteins, and the Enrico Fermis dreamed of when they worked out the theory that matter is energy; that a way to release that energy could give man almost unlimited amounts of power with which to do things. Those earlier atomic scientists saw the atom as a source of unlimited power to be used for human good. They hoped eventually to use atomic power directly, a goal the world has not yet attained.

Except in the explosion of an atomic or hydrogen bomb, the tremendous energy of the atom is not yet used directly. In today's nuclear reactors, a controlled thermonuclear reaction gives off heat, which then is used instead of coal and oil, under boilers, to produce steam to run wheels and generators that then give electricity. That use of atomic energy hardly taps the power in the atom.

The atom can become the same equalizer in peace that it promises to become in war. That gaseous centrifuge put out by the Degussa Company in West Germany turns out uranium 235. That means uranium 235 can be made to loose its full power on granite, to convert it to iron and the many other raw materials now uselessly locked up in it; to desalt water to irrigate the earth, to bridge the gap between the satisfied and dissatisfied peoples of the world.

CHAPTER 11

What Do We Do With the Big Machine?—I

SOME OF THE COSTLIEST, most disastrous events in human history have been caused by a problem sociologists call "cultural lag." It is a time problem. Throughout history it has always taken time for people to catch up with the facts of their day. The British, in an example already cited, were forced to admit, near the end of the Middle Ages, that shields and suits of armor were no protection against cannonballs and gunpowder. It was a hard-learned lesson, but not a lasting one. A few centuries later, on other battlefields, cultural lag again played a very costly part in British history.

The part was played during the Passchendaele campaign in France, in the Great War of 1914-1918. Lord Haig, commander of Britain's Overseas Expeditionary Force, was a brilliant student of military history. In the tradition of many leading military men, he could re-create many of the great battles and campaigns of history, Hannibal's, Caesar's, Napoleon's, Wellington's. In the best of that historical tradition Lord Haig lined his men up, row on row, and sent them in against the German positions. But the Germans were equipped with a new weapon called the machine gun, and the British soldiers dropped and died in huge numbers. General Haig suddenly realized that World War I was not conforming to his conception of the way a war *ought* to be fought. General Lord Haig was the victim of "cultural lag."

In our own American history, one of the most notable examples of cultural lag occurred late in 1929. It was the crash of the American stock market, and the beginning of the Great Depression of the Thirties. It would be a mistake to say that nobody in America knew that a depression was on its way, or that a stock market collapse was imminent. Months before, several economists and investment experts had sounded this warning. But these men were among the few in every age who are not behind the facts of their time. The names? They included Roger Babson, the economist and stock analyst; Charles Merrill, who later founded the nation's largest investment house; Bernard Baruch, and Joseph P. Kennedy. Those men saw and understood the financial facts of their time. They got out of the stock market, and they saved their fortunes by doing so.

They were not secretive about their actions. Babson and Merrill, in particular, told thousands of people that the market would break. Babson published his beliefs so that millions could read them. But very few Americans heeded these warnings. Most Americans believed prosperity was a permanent fixture. But the big machine broke down. Soon seventeen million Americans were without steady work.

That Great Depression hit us a few years after eight million Germans found themselves without work, and there were three million Englishmen in the same boat. So was most of the world.

Most Americans know something about the Great Depression, but not what caused it, or what ended it. World War I was the main cause; World War II was the main cure. People do not eat and wear and use as much as quickly in peacetime as they blow up and destroy in wartime. Factories that expanded to produce for a world war in 1914 had to shrink back to peacetime production in 1919. The number of jobs decreased immediately after the war, and this cutback grew directly into the Great Depression a few years later. It was felt first in Germany. It ended there first, too, when Adolf Hitler put eight million unemployed Germans to work turning out guns instead of butter. The economy really began booming in Germany after 1933, as the German part of the big machine was prepared for war.

In 1936, the Civil War in Spain, the intervention by fascists, Nazis, and communists, was a sign of things to come for some Americans. Jobs suddenly became less scarce in America after the Spanish Civil War. Then, after Pearl Harbor, there was no job shortage at all in the United States. War brought prosperity.

It would be hard to measure what this solution for the problems of the big machine cost the human race in World War II. Our share of the cost was more than three hundred billion dollars in four years. And the cost in lives. What is the value in money of the lives of Americans who died that way? Or what is the value in money of the other fifty million lives that were snuffed out in World War II?

In time of peace all men on earth, except those hungry for power, will agree that war is evil; that war should somehow be prevented. Men can agree to this idea most readily and willingly when a war has just ended; when even the victors are nearly exhausted; when the inevitable selfish demands of one nation have not yet begun to arouse the suspicions of another; and when the preparations for a new war have not yet started.

Precisely this kind of concern about the failure of the world's economic machine and distaste for war brought the nations of the world together in September, 1946, for a fateful conference in Copenhagen, Denmark. Those who attended hoped to resolve the greatest problems of mankind by facing some of the most important facts of their day.

They gathered in Copenhagen to prevent a costly and dangerous bit of history from repeating itself. Representatives of twenty nations attended this conference to talk about ways to solve what they thought would be the world's main problems after World War II. All the big industrial nations except the Soviet Union were there. All the big food importing countries were there too. No conference in this century was more important to the world than this one; not because it did what it tried to do, but because it failed. It did not prevent history from repeating itself.

The men who attended that conference were not troubled by cultural lag. They recognized the facts of their time, fifteen years ago. They included the late Fiorello La Guardia and Herbert Hoover. Those men knew that most of the world was hungry; that many countries were producing less food than before the war, yet had to feed more people. Most of the world was poverty-stricken. There was much unrest which could lead to revolution. The world's economies were shaken; there was fear of depression in the industrial countries. Something had to be done.

To deal with the facts, a three-point program was drawn up:

First, deal with the world's food problem by doubling the food supply through a twenty-five-year program.

Second, put the factories and manufacturing plants of the industrial nations to work turning out the technological things needed to make the program work. This move alone would require more industrial output than went into fighting World War II.

Third, begin a world-wide search for raw materials to meet the needs of factories producing for exploding populations.

Do these things, said the delegates in Copenhagen, and disarmament conferences would never again be necessary.

But the Copenhagen Conference failed. The result of that failure led directly to the series of high defense budgets in America, and the series of disarmament conferences in Geneva that have made so many headlines in recent years. It is a costly, and dangerous repeat performance of history.

It is costly because behind the two big power blocs are invested hundreds of billions of dollars, rubles, francs, and pounds in destructive power. The total breaks down to about ten tons of dynamite for every man, woman and child on this planet.

It is dangerous, because the poverty-stricken peoples are still poverty-stricken, food shortages remain, and unrest has carried revolution right to our front door.

The important question, then, is to discover why that Copenhagen Conference failed.

The answer is that neither the Soviet Union nor the United States wanted the Copenhagen Conference to succeed. The American delegate said, during the final session, that while the goals of the conference were noble and worthwhile, it was a fact that no government was prepared to give either money or authority to any international organization over which it did not have full control.

What he meant was that America would not support the plan.

No Soviet delegate was there to say anything because, then as now, it is not in the Soviet Union's interest to see any strong international organization established to stabilize the world as it is. That is what the Copenhagen Conference tried to do. The Soviet Union did not attend because the U.S.S.R. wants to see the world changed into a communist one.

Since the day that we helped wreck that conference, the world has indeed changed; to a great extent as the Soviets hoped. Compare any world map of 1946 with one today. See for yourself how much territory the communists have gained since 1946. Consider the problems that existed in those territories for communists to exploit in gaining power.

What Americans did at that Copenhagen Conference, or rather what our representatives did not do, was prompted by cultural lag. Lord Haig did not understand the kind of war he was in, so he lost battles until he learned. Too many Americans, whose patriotism is rooted in their blood and emotions instead of in their minds, make it clear that they do not understand the kind of war we have been in since 1918.

In that year the Soviet Union put Marxism to work to prove, by whatever means necessary, that its system was the best for all men, politically, economically, socially, and philosophically. Today's unthinking Americans, long on anticommunist noise but very short on anticommunist knowledge, will cause us to lose our battles until they catch up with the facts of our time.

One such fact, vital to us, is that the United States no longer has a "national economy." If you doubt this, visit almost any part of the world today. Go to the Middle East, for example.

In the Middle East only a few short years ago, thanks to bilharziasis, tuberculosis, malaria, intestinal flukes, and the diseases and effects of hunger and malnutrition, people were increasing in number at a rate around one per cent a year. Now the population increases by about three per cent a year.

What happened?

What happened goes back to American medical and chemical laboratories, back to American international economic interests and commitments. The answer lies in tubes and vials of antibiotics, sulfa drugs and other medicines. Traveling medical teams, made up of local doctors, many of them trained in American medical schools, have used these products to keep much of the world alive today.

If, for any reason, the output of American medicines were to stop, or even be interrupted, the death rate in most of the world around us would rise almost at once. If laboratories in the United States, in Britain, in the U.S.S.R., in Germany, and other advanced, developed nations were to be destroyed in war, it would be safe to say that at least half the populations of the so-called backward, underdeveloped countries would die.

So we arrive again at another of the most important facts of our time. For the first time in history, the world cannot survive the war being discussed at such length in the Geneva disarmament talks. Wars have been called obsolete before in human history, but not for the same reasons. War is useless at this point in history. It will not make us secure. It will not keep the world out of the hands of communism.

The world moved out of Og's Stone Age, perhaps ten thousand years ago. Since Og's time, men have lived through the different ages of metal, through the ages of agriculture, through the Industrial Age—right up to our Age of Science. As the level of human technology improved, so did weapons. Each new weapon became more destructive than the last. They have all been used, too.

It is possible that man will fight again in the Age of Science, but it is doubtful if he will live to fight again after that. He won't come out of the next war, and go on to bigger and better things as he did before. Albert Einstein, whose ideas about matter and energy helped to get us into this position, was once asked if he knew what the weapons of World War III might be like. Dr. Einstein said that he did not know what weapons man would develop before a possible World War III, but he did know what the weapons after that war would be. The weapons would be stone axes and spears, he said, and soldiers' uniforms would be animal skins.

Reporters at that meeting thought Einstein was joking. Einstein had never been more serious. Reporters at that meeting suffered from cultural lag. They were not thinking about the changing bases of power that are the starkly new facts of our time; as new as today's petroleum engineer, for example.

Petroleum engineering is not what it was in the old days. Mass spectrometers and electronic sounding equipment are now used to locate new oil wells. Wells are driven down more than twelve thousand feet. That routine calls for very different tools and methods of drilling than were used in Nineteenth Century Pennsylvania when an engineer named Drake touched good oil at less than seventy feet. It did not cost much to get good oil at seventy feet. It is far more expensive and complicated to get it at twelve thousand feet.

Consequently, the modern petroleum engineer and his work are the products of a very complicated and highly developed industry. That word "complicated" is meaningful for our future.

It requires about six years of training, at a good university as well as on the job, to turn out today's petroleum engineer. All that training and experience is necessary because there are no oil deposits to be found at depths of seventy feet any more, anywhere on earth. All that training and experience is necessary now to maintain the United States as the great world power we are. But, in a way few understand, that need makes us a vulnerable world power too; far more vulnerable than in the days, not so long ago, of America's last military action: the Korean War in the early 1950s. The Chinese troops we fought then came from a poorly developed nation. Red China did not have many factories, nor much electric or other power, to back up its manpower. China's high-powered weapons came from Russia. But if that scene shifted to some time after 1965, the scene would be quite different. By then, communist China will be turning out its own atomic bombs. Its nuclear reactors are already producing the critical parts needed to make the bomb. And in Northwest China, outside its science center near Lanchow, the Chinese government has built a ballistic missiles plant.

Combine these two Space Age weapons in Chinese hands, as they will be by 1965. Add to that a long-range suicide bomber force. Then do what many Americans urged during the Korean affair: Cross the Yalu River and bomb Red China, knowing that Red China would bomb American territory in return.

In that kind of give-and-take bombing, which country would suffer more: a highly developed, very complicated, industrial America, or a still poorly developed, relatively uncomplicated, mainly agricultural communist China? Which country would survive heavy damage best? How many diabetics, for example, are alive today in China because of insulin produced in Chinese drug houses? How many diabetics do our pharmaceutical houses keep alive in America? Which population depends more on its science and technology for its well-being and survival? What do you do in your home, when the power fails? How do you cook and provide heat, and light, and power for washing machines and refrigerator motors?

Communist China's leaders understand the importance of our complicated society as it relates to their plans to become the dominant world power. Their awareness of our complexity is the key to Red China's foreign policy today. As the last Soviet Communist Party Congress in Moscow showed, there is even basic disagreement in the communist world between a China that does not fear a nuclear war and a Russia that does.

But why should China fear nuclear war? What better way is there to assure the communist future China wants for the world than to weaken or destroy our complicated society? We have much to lose in such a war. China has little. What better time is there for nuclear war, when most Americans do not know that ours is no longer a national economy; that our part of the big machine, if employed to outgun, outship, and out-missile communism, cannot possibly stop it that way, or make us secure?

What men like General Lord Haig did not know about the machine gun in the world of World War I made it shape the problem of cultural lag in his day. What Americans, and most of the rest of the human race, do not know about technological man in the 1960s makes him shape that same problem in our time.

Most of the world, and this includes the Soviet Union, depends on technological man to produce goods from poorer and poorer qualities of raw materials in larger and larger amounts. To use poorer quality raw materials calls for more highly developed, more complicated and costly ways of mining, not the simple methods used in the days of the first factories. The world needs highly trained technical men and complicated, expensive equipment to dig raw materials from the ground. Those raw materials go off to factories which have specially built, expensive equipment to turn out the metals, and the chemicals, and the plastics, and the fabrics we ride in, dress in and live in. Technical superiority with a low quality, high cost, raw materials base is what spells power and prosperity in our world of the Sixties. This has produced very different realities for us to recognize in our time from those that earlier Americans faced when they developed these United States into a world power on a low-cost, high-quality resource base.

It would be impossible to maintain our kind of world without technicians, and the petroleum engineer is a prime example. He, and technicians like him, has made war obsolete, for the first time in history. His technology can disappear after the next war, as can all advanced technology. Under these conditions history can come full circle as Albert Einstein made clear: from the caveman back to the caveman.

Is this nonsense? Is it scare talk? Is it gloom and doom mongering? Not quite. Unskilled men began the Industrial Age with an oil well seventy feet deep into a high-quality oil field. The same kind of men began the Industrial Age by pushing shovels into high-quality iron ore and pushing picks into high-quality coal, just by scratching at the earth's surface.

These men began on a low-cost, high-quality base. That base is gone, used up.

Start a war today. Use the kind of bombs that can wipe out technicians and the universities that train them, and the factories and laboratories that give them the tools and methods they need to keep us in metals and plastics. Do that in all the technologically advanced countries, and then try to start over again, without technicians, without tools, without knowledge. Find out how it feels to live in a world where all the ready sources of vital materials have disappeared.

Several years ago, Liaquat Ali Khan, one of the chief leaders of Pakistan, said there could be no security for anyone as long as the world was divided into two parts. He did not have in mind communists and non-communists. He was speaking of the rich and the poor; the hungry and the well-fed; the gulf that Pope John XXIII spoke about to the Cuban people. He had in mind the same problem that those men failed to resolve at the Copenhagen Conference. What he had in mind poses a vital question for us now.

In light of the failure of the Copenhagen Conference; in the light of disarmament conferences that get nowhere in Geneva, and the continuing arms race, what do you suppose a visitor from outer space might think, someone with no earthly axes to grind, as he or it looked at all this? Would he get the idea that mankind was less interested in bettering human life, more interested in destroying it?

CHAPTER 12

What Do We Do With the Big Machine?—II

ON SEVERAL WALLS left standing among the ruins of ancient centers of civilization in the Middle East are the stories of those places, carved in stone to last forever. In each case those stone records tell the story of a confident people, proud of their power and sure of their future. There is nothing in those records to explain why "forever" did not last long for them as centers of civilization. There is nothing to explain why all that is left of those places today are impressive piles of stone.

There may be nothing in those stone records to answer that question, but there are a few things in the historical record to suggest what happened to some of those ancient people. Consider the events at a place called Mylae in the year 260 B.C., when the Carthaginians were knocked into the junk heap of history. What happened was the "corvus" incident. It changed warfare at sea.

The corvus was a simple gadget developed by the Romans.

152

It was a kind of ladder with hooks along the outer edge which could be dropped onto an enemy ship when it was close by. Roman marines would use it as a bridge to get at the enemy crew. This was not war as the Carthaginians had known and fought it, to become the leading naval power of their day. They went into that battle of Mylae confident in their power, sure of their future. They lost their future in that battle because they could not adjust their way of thinking to cope with the corvus. A new basis of power in sea warfare was thus established.

Involved in that incident was the age-old problem of cultural lag considered in the preceding chapter, plus another special ingredient. The same kind of special ingredient brontosaurus faced as a problem when dinosaurs ruled the earth about a hundred million years ago. We face it now. Brontosaurus could not solve that special problem, and it is one of the more important reasons why he and his kind no longer exist. He could not solve the problem of a body that grew faster than its brain and nervous system, to the point where the brain had very little control over the different parts of his body which was about seventy feet long and weighed thirty tons. Brontosaurus could be attacked somewhere in the rear, and literally be nibbled to death before his brain told him what was happening. One of the main reasons brontosaurus isn't around any more is that fact. His parts weren't tied together too well; his system of controls was poor.

That fact is a national problem for us today; not in terms of our bodies, but in terms of our way of life. Just as that dinosaur grew too fast, our society has been growing at a faster rate than our ability to control it. Proof that this is true can be found regularly in newspapers around the nation, carrying the story of another one of the most frustrating and serious matters we've had to face in our history.

Part of this particular story concerns what are now called the nation's chronically unemployed: people who cannot find jobs. Millions of Americans are unemployed despite the fact that our factories are pouring out more of everything today than ever before, at a time when our standard of living is higher than ever before.

It is a story in statistics which show that in 1958 we were turning out 35 per cent more of everything than we had produced ten years earlier, with eight hundred thousand less workers than had been employed in 1948. In that ten-year period America's population increased by more than twenty million persons while the number of jobs in manufacturing industries dropped by about a million. In the best, most prosperous time we have ever known, with a growing population, fewer jobs are available.

Yet in the back pages of our newspapers jobs are listed that are not being filled because there is a shortage of people to fill them. One advertisement calls for astrophysicists, another calls for systems engineers. There are jobs for technicians to handle infrared space instrumentation work, for men with training in geodetics. There are jobs, plenty of them. And there are unemployed, plenty of them.

Between them lies a gap which cannot be crossed by many of the chronic unemployed in the nation. The gap is there because machines have changed, and are changing, the world we live in. They have made the jobs of metalsmiths, plumbers, steamfitters, joiners, lathe operators, and dozens of others gradually obsolete.

The most important of those machines is the computer, the working brain of a new way of life; our way of life this minute. Without these machines, few of the things we take for granted would be possible. Computers run entire banks of machines which do, in a matter of minutes, the same job that, only a few years ago, took many workers many hours.

Machines have removed the human limit on production. No one really knows the machine's limits. But computers, and transfer machines, and automatic assembly lines make possible the six million automobiles we can buy today. If automobiles were produced today as they were before automatic machines entered our affairs, only the very rich could afford to buy them. Manpower is too expensive and too slow to turn out the number of cars Americans need and want, at the price most Americans feel they can afford to pay today.

Automation is part of our way of life. It makes possible telephone service as we know it today. The telephone industry was much different before automatic machines began to replace manpower. If the telephone companies were to handle today's number of phone calls the old way, every woman in our labor force would be employed by the telephone companies, and 20 per cent of the jobs in that industry would still not be filled. Manpower is too expensive and takes too much time to handle telephone calls as most Americans expect it to be done today.

In these ways, automatic machines are a double-edged problem. We cannot do without them. They are part of our way of life. But increasing numbers of Americans are finding that they cannot get jobs because of them.

Automation has changed the value and the place of labor, and the value and place of management and capital. Today's unemployed are less valuable as workers because the work they once did can be done better by machines. They will remain less valuable, and remain out of work until they somehow develop the kinds of skills automated America requires.

This does not mean that all steamfitters, or plumbers, or lathe operators must become astrophysicists or infrared instrumentation experts. It does mean that men must learn new skills needed to make them valuable again in new jobs being created by automation. That is the one way to bridge the gap.

The gap must be bridged or the chronically unemployed will become dangerous to the country's future—bitter symbols of the price paid for automation. Behind them, pressures will build up to hold off automation or to prevent its development.

This has already happened in a strike of the tugboat operators in New York City in 1960.

The tugboat operators were reacting against automation, against being displaced by machines that do the same work faster and better. Their fear and resentment spread quickly to railroad men who have also been losing out to machines. They, in turn, were supported by other labor groups on the docks who face the same problem.

The automation problem is serious for them right now. With no work, men earn no wages. With no wages they become a drain on the national economy. There is little dignity in unemployment insurance. Men need the jobs, not the dole.

Labor is not alone in its fear of automation. A recent survey by the Research Institute of America showed that management for the most part looks forward with resignation to automation, not with hope. Why? Because most existing plants and factories must be replaced. Many billions of dollars' worth of equipment in today's factories is already obsolete.

Both labor and management have good legitimate reasons for not looking forward with joy to an automated future. So did the Carthaginian generals and admirals have good legitimate reasons to oppose changing their ideas about sea power to meet the new challenge of the Roman corvus. In both instances, men were concerned about the cost of change. That concern cost Carthage its future.

That concern can cost America its future, if we ignore such challenging signs as the International Conference on Automation held in Moscow in June, 1959.

Western experts, including Americans, came away from that meeting impressed by the high quality of Soviet theories in this new field. Despite their reaction, there was not much in the reports of the conference published in the United States to suggest that they were particularly concerned about this. But they should have been concerned about its effect on our lives, because that Moscow conference touched the heart of

Soviet plans to become the leading world power in our time.

Mr. Khrushchev, on many occasions, has made this Soviet intention clear. For the most part, his remarks have not been taken seriously by most Americans. Most of us have thought that the Soviet Union would have to duplicate America's experience in building up an industrial power.

But Mr. Khrushchev was not thinking of that routine in the past, and he does not have it in mind now. He has been pushing an enormous, little-publicized Soviet effort to bypass our road to industrial power. His plan is to succeed through automation. He has no intention of waiting for Russian workers to match Americans in output. In regular Soviet industry today, where there is no automation, the average Soviet worker turns out about half as much as an American worker. In automated industries Soviet output matches our own.

On his visit to the United States in 1959, Mr. Khrushchev stated that sometime in the 1970s his country would both outproduce the United States and would have a higher standard of living. The fact is that through automation this can be done. Not because of Mr. Khrushchev's views on the subject but for the reason noted earlier, that no one really knows the machine limit on production.

This ignorance about the capacity of automated production was made quite clear several years ago in England, at Doncaster, where an automated factory was built to produce light bulbs. Eight specially designed machines were installed to help meet Britain's own needs and to produce for export. After putting the second of those machines into operation, the British discovered that they had underestimated the output of each machine. They did not need eight machines. Two machines, working twelve hours a day, turned out more light bulbs than the entire United Kingdom could use. Two machines replaced hundreds of workers who were needed to turn out those bulbs the old way.

No human hand touched that automated process. Sand and

other raw materials went into one end of this factory, and finished light bulbs packed in cartons came out the other end, where they were loaded automatically into railroad freight cars.

By using new, automated methods, the U.S.S.R. can bypass its serious problems of inept, inefficient labor, and with a small, well-trained labor force, Russia or any other country can increase its output enormously. That the Soviet Union is doing this was quite obvious at the Brussels World's Fair 1958, where Russia won the grand prize for its automated milling machine. The Russians outcompeted us and the other leading industrial nations.

There should be real cause for concern for Americans in the Soviet drive to automate its way into the future. There is, of course, the obvious meaning of an unfriendly Soviet industrial system able to produce goods of war as well as peace. But that is not a new problem. Our more important concern is that a real test is in the making between communism and democracy, to see which system can best meet the problems of automation.

Automation puts an enormous strain on the American way of life, as was pointed up by the then Secretary of the Treasury, George Humphrey, in 1955. Mr. Humphrey said then that except in a few isolated cases a man could no longer earn his living with his own two hands in this country. To produce the things Americans want now, to meet demands fast enough and cheaply enough, Americans must use specialized tools and specialized machines.

In discussing automation those words "cheaply enough" are important. Human labor is not cheap; not just in terms of the more than three dollars an hour that, for example, a steel worker gets today, but in any terms. Doncaster's automated light bulb factory is run by electrical power, and that kind of power can be delivered to that factory to be used by electric motors at a cost between one to four cents a horsepower hour.

If a horse were actually used to do an hour's work in that factory, to replace that electric motor, it would have to be rented for about seventy-five cents to a dollar and ten cents an hour. That means horse labor is thirty times as expensive as an electric motor for the same amount of work. The horse is out. Too expensive.

Consider human labor in comparison to that electric motor. A man can do in ten hours about as much physical labor as a horse can do in one hour. Assume that a man receives the average wage for an unskilled laborer in this country, between one dollar and a dollar and twenty-five cents an hour. That would mean ten to twelve and a half dollars a day for human labor, to do the same amount of physical labor a horse could do for a dollar and ten cents or the physical work that the electrical engine did for a few cents.

There you have the reason why Mr. Humphrey said that today's American can no longer do as his ancestors did in this land, earn his living with his own two hands. Raw human labor may one day be eliminated entirely, because it is too valuable to be used in the old way. Human beings are wasted doing work that can be done better and cheaper by automatic machines, with operational brains.

Operational brains do not think. That is the one job that remains for men to fill. Whatever machines can do today, whatever plans we may have for them tomorrow, they cannot yet replace brain power.

That kind of power is facing its hardest test in history in this Age of Automation, because automation has changed the value of the man, the individual, in our way of life. Not too long ago, a man's value was measured by what he could do with his hands to build and make things. The muscles of men and animals built early America, with simple uncomplicated tools. The more skilled a man was with his hands, the better the life he might enjoy. During that period of history we set up the political system under which we still live; the ecnomic system we still describe as based on private enterprise and individual initiative. But those systems are not the same in our time as they were then because, as Secretary Humphrey emphasized, the value of men and women is no longer measured the same way.

This was the real significance of that unpublicized event that took place in Port Arthur, Texas, back in mid-March, 1959, when the fully automated refining plant went into operation. That event moved us out of the world most of us still think we live in, and right into the Age of Automation. A technician flipped a switch to start this country's first fully automatic, computer-controlled industrial operation. A desk-sized operational brain, one computer, controls the most important steps of that oil operation. Before that event, computers worked out problems and controlled certain specific parts of a process, but not the process as a whole. It was described by those who accomplished it as only a pioneer project, but one with great significance for the future of automation. It is also of great importance for the future of the nation.

Automation is with us. It is another part of the new basis of power in our time, precisely as the corvus had been for the Romans and Carthaginians. It must be developed fully. There is no other choice if world leadership is to be part of our future.

It must be developed fully for another reason, also. It could be our means of solving, in our time and for our way of life, the problem brontosaurus could not solve in his time. Automation could be the answer to our need to produce more things, faster, for more people, and at the same time control the increasingly rapid growth of our increasingly complicated society. Our future will be an automated one.

CHAPTER 13

The Race: Moon vs. Survival

THE FIRST SPACE TRAVELERS setting out for Mars will travel at twenty-six miles a second for twenty-three days before landing on that planet.

We may see this happen within ten years, perhaps twenty. Billions upon billions of dollars and rubles will have gone into research to produce a single space craft powerful enough to carry two people, whatever equipment and supplies they need, and enough fuel to get them to Mars and back. Billions will go into research to devise a way to keep those two people alive as they pass through the layers of radiation around the earth and in space.

Some day, when fifty satellites are placed in permanent orbit above the earth's surface, properly spaced at exactly the right altitudes, it will be possible to beam television programs to receivers anywhere on earth. It will be possible to telephone anybody anywhere. In a few years rockets will carry passengers from New York to London in fifteen minutes. Moscow will be only twenty-five minutes away, and Jakarta in Indonesia, half around the world from New York, will be thirty-five to forty minutes away.

Men will place transparent steel bubbles on the moon, Mars, and Venus, and colonies of human beings will push the human frontier into the solar system. Inside those steel bubbles, oxygen, nitrogen and the rest of the gases will be released from the elements to make air to breathe. From such bases man will be off to the star clusters billions of miles away.

This is man's future. The wildest imaginings of what used to be called science fiction are possible in time, through science and technology.

Space travel, space life, are part of the predictions many leading rocket scientists are making about the kind of world we can expect in twenty-five years. They see a limitless future for the human race.

It would take a brave man to challenge what those scientists see twenty-five years ahead. Recall life twenty-five years ago and try to imagine the kind of world you would then have expected to live in today. How many of the one hundred and twenty-six million Americans alive in the 1930s believed that television, plastics, sulfa drugs and antibiotics, transistors, jet and rocket power, and atomic energy would be realities in their lifetimes? Half the products coming out of American manufacturing plants today were unknown twenty-five years ago. Who, then, would dare to say that the next twenty-five years will not see more accomplishments every bit as remarkable?

One man who dares to contradict those rocket scientists is the Swedish writer and economist Gunnar Myrdal. Myrdal worked with United Nations economic commissions all over the world. A few years ago he wrote a book called *Rich Lands and Poor,* which stressed the fact that the future could very easily be anything *but* the kind of place those rocket scientists predicted.

The danger to our future, he said, lies in the completely changed dimensions of time and survival. Science alone will not guarantee or secure the future of the human race. It is what we do with science that will decide our future.

How so?

In a laboratory a short time before World War II began, a chemist poured some pentamethyleneamine into a glass container, mixed in a quantity of sebacic acid, then added some xylenols—and stepped back to watch the world change a little. That successful experiment had begun thirteen years earlier. It cost the Du Pont company twenty million dollars before that chemist succeeded. But it was worth it. He had produced nylon.

In another chemical laboratory, shortly after World War II, a company closed the books on another experiment which could have changed the world even more, if it had succeeded. The result might have turned poor soils into good soils. For an overpopulated agricultural world this would have been a blessing. The experiment failed. It took eleven years and its cost also ran into the millions of dollars. After eleven years the company gave up.

It took thirty years to develop the Diesel engine. It took more than thirty years to produce the first modern gas turbine. In those few examples, science and technology, given enough money, produced results—given enough time. This has been the story of the past twenty-five years, which gave us the world we inhabit, from televison sets to earth satellites.

In most of America's years as a nation, we and the people before us have lived in a special environment. There are not many people on earth who can show their way of life in terms of constant economic growth that has always risen faster than their population growth. We in these United States can.

America's population grew rapidly, particularly in the late Nineteenth and early Twentieth Centuries. But American industry always stayed ahead, turning out more food, shoes, bicycles, can openers, and battleships each year.

This nation grew richer with time, and more powerful.

Even yesterday's wars did not change this growth. Even wars were a shot in the arm to our economy. America produced so much wealth in peacetime that we could destroy or give away billions of dollars' worth of goods, over three hundred billion dollars' worth in World War II alone, and still have enough left to maintain national growth. During the worst of our wars, Americans dug raw materials out of mines, pumped them out of wells, harvested them off the land, and fed the factories, which were always worked by enough hands. Even during the worst of our wars, America produced so much of so many things that the nation went on growing richer and stronger.

The key to this accomplishment lies in the fact that our population has never grown faster than our economy, for any significant time. We could produce more of all things than we needed. We piled up wealth. We were unique in our world. Few peoples throughout history have known that experience. Few peoples have ever been treated as kindly by history and geography.

This accounted for the wealth needed yesterday to pay for the research and development of nylons, plastics, Diesels and gas turbines. It accounts for the money available now to pay for the research and development of rockets powerful enough to send an American off to Mars.

All through American history, from Benjamin Franklin fiddling with kites and electricity, through Edison fiddling with light bulbs and phonographs, to Einstein fiddling with the nature of the universe, Americans have had time and money to work out scientific problems and to become rich and powerful.

That was American history, but the American picture has

changed in a little understood, but critically important way.
A way that is little understood because in times called prosperous there are millions of persons unemployed.

One of the most important facts of our time is this nation's
need for all the trained hands and brains it can get, regardless
of race or creed. We need them if we are to produce enough,
and if our economy is to grow enough, in the next ten years to
make the money for the research that will keep this nation a
great power in the Space Age.

Training all the Americans who could possibly be trained
would add only ten per cent more people to the nation's labor
force in the next ten years. But, to maintain our economic
growth our labor force will need fifty per cent more goods and
services in that time. A manpower shortage lies ahead for us,
just ahead of the news that four million persons were unemployed at the beginning of the 1960s. We have already pointed
out many problems to tackle in the next ten years, but none
of them is more important than this one. It is another of our
basic economic problems.

As many Americans see it, we live in the best of all possible
worlds. You are one of more than one hundred and ninety
million potential borrowers of money from an American
banker. You are one of one hundred and ninety million potential customers for an American storekeeper. You may be one of
the one hundred and ninety million souls an American clergy-
man sees in the nation's parishes and congregations. And at
the end of every year, you will be joined by three million
more potential borrowers, buyers, and Bible readers than
there were at the start of the year.

Butcher, baker, or candlestick-maker, Americans agree on
the desirability of a growing population. We can read about it
in most economics textbooks published in this country since
1900. There is a definite tie between the good life and a growing population. In 1900, for example, seventy-five million
Americans lived in a land where streets were paved with

gold, at least as far as the other people in the world were concerned. Fifty years later, twice as many Americans were living better than ever.

We are making more money than ever before. You may have two cars in your garage. You may even own two houses. And our rocket scientists say we haven't seen anything yet. Twenty-five years in the future two hundred fifty-five million Americans will have richer lives than today's Americans can even imagine. The more people, the merrier, as we see it.

What we see in this respect is not a vision shared by most of the human race. An Egyptian, for example, would not agree that he lived in the best of all possible worlds. His world is not made merrier by more people. Quite the contrary. Because there are more people, he is not living as well today as he did twenty years ago. Egypt's population has grown, too, but with no sign that it spells the good life, as we see it. Instead, there are twenty-five million people in Egypt today, and practically all of them are poorer than fewer Egyptians were twenty-five years ago.

Why this difference?

In Egypt, people have been turning out goods more slowly than Americans. The population in Egypt has grown, and is growing, faster than the economy. That difference measures poverty, not wealth. For this reason, the Egyptian is not particularly interested in who gets to the moon first. His concern is closer to home, in the problem of growing poverty in an overcrowded country. It is the main concern of most of the human race.

Historians have worked long and hard to discover the reasons for the wars that have periodically decimated the human race. No answer has ever been more important than the Egyptian's; growing poverty in an overcrowded country.

The Egyptian, then, is dangerous; as hungry, dissatisfied people have always been dangerous. But such people are particularly dangerous to our future because such dissatisfaction can explode in revolution and war. It could spread to the nuclear destruction of half the world. Where does *that* put the future? There is not much chance that American history would repeat itself. It has already been pointed out that our way of life could not survive nuclear war, any more than the Soviet Union's could.

The leaders of both countries know that nuclear war has gone far beyond the American, or the Soviet public's understanding. For example, Mr. Khrushchev's atomic technicians have made something close to a hundred-megaton bomb. This means that the time is not far off when man will build a thousand-megaton bomb. It is mainly a technological problem. Rocket science has reached the point where the ballistic missile to carry this huge bomb can be built. Nuclear war becomes obsolete with that weapon. Imagine a triangle, touching on Chicago in the west, with the broad end between Boston and Washington, D. C., in the east. In that triangle lies the overwhelming bulk of America's industrial power. Most of our technical training schools and institutions, and many of our best universities and colleges, are located in that area. Most of our population lives there too.

On the other side of the world, in the Soviet Union, a similar, though lopsided triangle touches on Leningrad, in the north. Its broad end touches on the Black Sea and the Caspian Sea in the south. Within that area lies the overwhelming bulk of Soviet industrial power. Most of Russia's best technical training schools and institutes are in that triangle. Most of the Soviet Union's population lives there too.

Now take just a single thousand-megaton bomb. Don't worry about aiming it accurately. That's not necessary with such a bomb. If you were in the U.S.S.R., you would send it somewhere north of Pittsburgh at an altitude of about three hundred miles. When that bomb exploded there would be little left of life or wealth in a ten-state area that reaches from Illinois to Connecticut, and from Michigan to the Carolinas. The industrial heart of America would be destroyed.

You can do the same thing to the U.S.S.R. by exploding a thousand-megaton bomb somewhere south of Moscow, at three hundred miles altitude.

If that happened neither you nor the Russians would have much hope of putting man in space.

That kind of future, of revolution and war, can be a stronger possibility for the world twenty-five years from now than the one our rocket scientists predicted. Because revolution and war are inevitable in a world in which the rich lands keep growing richer and the poor lands keep growing poorer. That is what Gunnar Myrdal wrote. His words must be considered.

Our space scientists, and those of the Soviet Union, England, or any other nation, need time to work out the scientific and technical problems involved in putting a man deep into space. They need money. Both needs can be met in an environment of peace. It is a simple fact that neither can be met in an environment of modern war.

The key to man's future in space, then, lies in a critically important way with the Egyptians, the Laotians, the Latin Americans and the other poor people of the world. What they do will do more to decide whether the future brings peace or war than anything rich Americans or increasingly rich Russians may do. What do you suppose the future will bring if the twin problems of poverty and exploding populations continue unsolved; if dissatisfied people bring about the kind of revolution you found one morning on your doorstep in Cuba?

Could a free, rich America collect the future our rocket scientists predicted in such a revolutionary environment? Could America stay free, or rich, in that environment?

Our rocket scientists made their predictions about the limitless future for the human race in *The Journal of the American Rocket Society* in 1959. Their prediction covered a twenty-five-year period. That means the predictions will stand or fall by 1984. And by an interesting coincidence 1984 is the title of the book we referred to in Chapter Five, by George Orwell. Remember, Orwell also made some predictions for that year. As he saw 1984, however, people like our rocket scientists had spent too much time trying to solve the problems of man in space, and not enough time solving the problems of man on earth.

George Orwell's predictions do not show man headed for the stars. In Orwell's future, world governments have all become dictatorships. There are no rich nations any more. There is no freedom either, as we refer to freedom. Because Orwell's man did not find a way to use science to solve man's earthly problems. Orwell's man did not find that growing population led to a merrier world, or the good life.

In Orwell's 1984, the price of overpopulation is paid by the whole world. Babies were born faster than science could work out ways to feed, house, and clothe them. There were not enough raw materials to go around. To give everybody a fair share, new kinds of governments were established which controlled the use of everything, not unlike the early communist idea about controlled use and controlled consumption of things.

In Orwell's world there is no private enterprise, no individual initiative, and no individual dignity either. All that we now consider to be good about our way of life by then has vanished. Even Love is forbidden, as a birth control measure. There is little humanity left in Orwell's 1984.

Orwell never said it flatly but he made it quite clear that freedom, and governments based on the idea of freedom, cannot live without elbow room, without enough raw materials and production to go around.

George Orwell's view of science does not agree with that of our rocket scientists. He did not see science as the road to a limitless future. Most Americans, among the most satisfied and best fed people on earth, have the comfortable idea that it is only a matter of time until some kind of answer will be worked out by scientists in laboratories to solve the problems of the dissatisfied and poorly fed peoples. Most of us seem to have the idea that slide rules and test tubes can turn out miracles on demand.

It is easy, of course, to have faith in a better future when one has a full stomach and is set to wait out the future well-clothed, in a warm house. Unfortunately, more than 80 per cent of our neighbors in the world are not that well set up to last through the waiting period. They cannot solve their problems today on the miracles we expect from science in ten or twenty years. They can be dead long before that.

George Orwell sees those poor people shaping a grim future for us. Our rocket scientists see science shaping a brilliant future. How do you see it?

CHAPTER 14

What Went Wrong?

NO GROUP OF PEOPLE, anywhere, or at any time in history, have ever been able to live out their lives on their own terms. In all places, and at all times, people have been influenced by what was happening around them. No small number have been destroyed by those happenings.

This is not a well-known or generally understood fact of human history for most Americans. Until very recently, we had no real reason to be overly concerned about what happened around us in the rest of the world. Our main concern was always to be left alone to follow our own interests. We are among the very few people in history who were able to enjoy that luxury. We enjoyed it until World War II. After World War II we no longer enjoyed the privilege of minding our own business. We have considered some of the reasons for this in earlier chapters. Another of the principal reasons that we no longer have the ordered and controlled world we lived in until 1941 happened in December of that year, when the empire powers either lost, or gave up their empires. Suddenly, we could no longer deal with places like India, Burma, and Malaya, through the foreign offices of our close friends in Britain. Suddenly, we could no longer deal with the Dutch East Indies through our good friends in Holland, or with the African Congo through Belgium. Suddenly the world was no longer ordered or controlled by our friends, and we had to deal with it directly, not through people who shared our history, and culture, and sometimes even our language. Suddenly, we discovered that we could not live our lives on our own terms, either. We were pulled into the mainstream of history, and it has not been a familiar or a comfortable place to be.

It has been uncomfortable for us to the tune of about a hundred billion dollars in defense and technical assistance to keep the world the kind of place in which we could remain a free people. While John Q. American did not understand that effort when it began, and too many do not understand it yet, those defense and assistance programs were our counter-influence against the pressures of a rapidly changing world. It is time Americans understood that counter-influence for the vital part it has played from the beginning. It is one of our main weapons in a very different struggle from any we have known in our history. A struggle for survival.

As a counter-influence it hasn't worked too well right from the start. Something went wrong in most of the places where we tried it: from China, through Indo-China, to Laos and Cuba. What went wrong in those places which are now under communist influence?

What went wrong is part of a story that begins on a side street in the city of Milwaukee, Wisconsin, in the month of October, 1959. On that side street a team of reporters from one of the nation's top magazines was carrying out a survey. It was one of several similar teams operating around the country

to determine what people thought about our future. They
wanted to know what Americans expected in that future.

The 1950s had been an incredible ten years. Men had
climbed the highest mountain on earth. Others measured the
deepest parts of the ocean. Men took their first step into space.
Science was changing the physical world, and ideas were
changing the political world. Where would it all end? Where
should it end?

Wherever it ended, a Milwaukee housewife said to one of
those reporters, it should not end by changing things too much.
"I just want things to go on as they have been," she said.

As things had been? For that housewife and much of this
nation, the facts are as follows:

With an annual income of nine thousand dollars, her family
of five lived nicely in their twenty-one-thousand-dollar Cape
Cod house; and they could expect to continue to live nicely
for sixty or seventy years. That would be true provided that
nothing unexpected came along. That nine-thousand-dollar
income spelled three good meals a day, health insurance coverage, warm clothes, an automobile, and the good life.

But somewhat removed from that good life in Milwaukee
was Wong Ho who lived in a hovel in a Chinese city. He helped
turn China into a communist country in 1949.

Wong's income in 1945 was less than a hundred dollars a
year. His family of four did not live well. Wong's wife had
borne six children, but only two lived for more than five years.
As recently as 1955, more than five years after the communists
took over China, the Chinese communist delegates to the
Bandung Conference said they hoped they would be able to
lower the death rate among Chinese children. In 1955, half of
all children born on mainland China died before they were
five years old.

If hunger did not kill off Wong Ho's children, disease did.
They ate less than one square meal a day. They lived in mud-

walled, thatch-roofed huts, without good clothing. Wong Ho did not see the future the way that housewife in Milwaukee saw it. Wong had little reason to "want things to go on as they had been." He wanted things to change radically. Today communist science is changing his physical world, and communist ideas are changing his political world, along with the worlds of almost a billion of his neighbors.

.Communist science and communist ideas are at work in China, Laos, Indo-China, and Cuba, to change those worlds and ours. The housewife in Milwaukee and the business executive in Los Angeles, and the union worker at Cape Canaveral, and the farmer in Oregon, all want much the same things from the future. That fact is quite clear from the statistics. They show that most Americans are well satisfied with the way things have been going and are going now, and want them to continue as they are.

This is an impossible dream. The fact that it exists as it does suggests why things have gone wrong in the world around us, and why they may continue to go wrong.

It is an unfortunate fact that the science and the political ideas of the democratic nations are not now the leading forces in deciding the world's future. Western ideas were not the leading forces in China in 1949, or in Indo-China in 1954. They are not the most important ideas in Laos or Cuba right now.

In April, 1961, President Kennedy told the American Society of Newspaper Editors, the Milwaukee housewife, and the nation that we are facing a climax in our history. That climax concerns survival, he said; whether or not we will be a free people with democratic institutions in the future.

This was strong talk for Americans, who as recently as October, 1959, saw our future as nothing more than a continuation of our past.

How did President Kennedy happen to deliver such a strong and shocking talk to Americans in the spring of 1961, just two years after the Milwaukee survey in which Americans found themselves living in the best of all possible worlds?

The story can be told in terms of the important American newspapers published in New York City. One of them, *The New York Times,* is known all over the world. It has recently become our first truly national newspaper by opening a printing plant on the West Coast. Now Americans in San Francisco, and Los Angeles, and Portland, and Seattle can read *The New York Times* on the morning of publication, if they choose.

Is that important? Visit our embassies just about any place on earth and you will find that newspaper. It is read by the leaders of nearly every government on earth. They depend on it for the most complete coverage of events in this country. I have found copies of this paper in the offices of most of our senators and congressmen; in the offices of most of the agency heads I have visited in the nation's capital. They depend on it for news of other parts of the world. For years the *Times* has been spelling out plainly the ABCs of what went wrong from China through Cuba. But fewer people read *The New York Times* than read New York's tabloids. The tabloids are not known all over the world. They will not be found in many, if any, of our embassies. They are not read by many, if any, of the leaders of governments anywhere. Not that there are no facts in them. There are, in detail; facts aplenty about what goes on in bedrooms, brothels, and bars, from Chicago to Cairo. Those newspapers carried little or nothing to explain what went wrong in China or in Cuba to bring us to the point of President Kennedy's strong talk about the plain fact of survival for the nation.

More than three times as many Americans read the tabloids, the daily score cards of rapes and boozers, as go through the *Times*' detailed stories.

How come? Why are there so few good, top quality papers like *The New York Times* in the nation? And why so many tabloids which divert, amuse, and dabble in drivel? How can that housewife in Milwaukee be expected to know what is going on and what went wrong any place, if there are so few papers to tell her?

The answer, said a newspaper editor friend of mine in Hartford, Connecticut, is that the housewife prefers the tabloid type of paper. And he went through the record of newspaper failures to prove his point.

A tabloid rarely goes broke. A newspaper is a business, my editor friend said, like any other business. First of all, it has to survive. It cannot survive without public support.

Where is that public support for newspapers? What kind of programs do people support on television? What kind of books and magazines are best-sellers throughout the nation?

Well, a nation is like a business, too, in that it has to survive, first of all. This nation cannot survive without the right kind of public support for positive programs, in government and out of it, which will make the science and ideas of the democracies the weapons with which to fight for the future we want.

Before speaking to those newspaper editors, President Kennedy conferred with Prime Minister Macmillan. They examined the state of the world and found it to be critical in March, 1961. Never before in the history of the free peoples of the world had the need for unity against a common danger to the future of freedom been greater, these men said. Never before had the need to sacrifice for freedom been greater. The key word in this announcement was "sacrifice." It was the frustrating word in that announcement, too. Sacrifice what? Sacrifice to do what? Sacrifice how? Sacrifice where? Sacrifice why?

Since the end of World War II, when the West first realized that things were "going wrong," there have been few more overworked words in the English language than "sacrifice," and few more misunderstood words. Explaining that word in detail would mean telling that Milwaukee housewife that there is no way to make things "go on as they have been."

"Things as they have been" have brought us to a point in our affairs where Americans spend 30 per cent of their money on things they do not really need: extra television sets, extra automobiles, extra telephones, extra radios—our luxuries. But at this very minute, in places like the farming communities of Egypt, the people have no extras. All they have is less food to eat than ever before. It is impossible for them to visualize, much less understand, our extras. What the exploding populations of practically all of Asia, Africa and Latin America need are better steel plows with moldboards, better water pumps and shovels for ditch irrigation, better fertilizers and seed stock for larger crop yields.

One of the least understood facts of our life this minute is that freedom cannot exist in an unfree world; or at least that what we mean by freedom is impossible in an unfree world.

Many of the things that make it possible for us to pour 30 to 40 per cent of all the money we earn into luxuries come from the non-communist parts of the world. A communist China doesn't send to us the things needed to build television sets and radios. Neither does a communist Indo-China, or a communist Cuba. In Cuba, the important nickel-cobalt processing plant at Moa Bay is producing nickel-cobalt for the U.S.S.R. and communist China. Moa Bay was built by American money, to produce nickel and cobalt for jet engines and can openers for Americans. Now Moa Bay is producing a challenge to our way of life, instead.

In order to meet that challenge, consider taking that 30 to 40 per cent of all the money we spend now on things we do not really need, and spending it on the things we do need to survive; such things as better plows and moldboards for peasants from Bolivia to Burma; better fertilizers and seed stock for the exploding populations from Laos to Luanda. Consider using that part of our national income to influence the world our way; to help them find non-communist answers for their future, and ours.

Do you know what it would mean to put that much American science and technology to work to meet the challenge of communism?

What, for example, would happen to the thousands of jobs now tied up in turning out luxuries? What would happen to the electricians, the mechanics, the advertisers, public relations men, lawyers, shopkeepers, truck drivers, and salesmen, whose lives are tied in to that 30 per cent of all you buy? Would they be willing to retrain themselves to work at machines that make plows? Would they retrain themselves to work in chemical plants turning out fertilizers? Would some become agricultural workers to turn out seed stock, or mechanics to make irrigation pumps? Would *you* do this? Is anyone you know eager to make this sacrifice?

Taken out of the vaguely worded pronouncements made regularly by the heads of western states about "sacrifices," the above is one example of what that word implies when it is analyzed in detail. It would be a small part of the cost of survival, but even the most courageous political leaders have not yet admitted this to the American people.

Nevertheless, small sacrifices—practical ones—are important in correcting "what went wrong" since World War II. For instance, small sacrifices that we could make at the local, public, private, or parochial school down the block in our neighborhoods right now, to insure a future of freedom for our children.

It is easy to join a national movement to save the world from communism, or whatever. It is the harder, however (because it is more demanding), to join with the people of our community in an effort to save through our schools only a small part of the world in which our children will live. Let's say the Burmese part, for example.

Now, you make this decision for more than just Christian or humanitarian reasons. Off in upper Burma are the Bowdwin Mines, among the richest lead-nickel-zinc producers in Asia outside the communist territories. Quite a few factories in Western Europe, which keep our allies strong in peace and war, depend on those Burmese mines.

You decide that Burma is to be your community's project. You introduce Burmese languages into the fifth and sixth grades of your local school. You add courses in Burmese history, economics, and culture in the local high school. Then, one day, from the schools of your community come trained, qualified young people, the kind the Peace Corps will be able to call on to insure that democratic ideas and democratic science will become the strongest driving forces in the world. They must be the strongest forces if we are to survive as a free people. Your government can use this kind of help, which you can give.

The United States Information Agency can use your help. It has carried on a much neglected people-to-people, sister-cities program for years, to do the same job. So you decide, right there in your town, that Rangoon, Burma, will be your sister city. You set up a student exchange program. You bring young Burmese to your school for several terms, and you send your sons and daughters to Rangoon for their schooling. In this way, Burma learns about America and Americans learn about Burma. You set up a management exchange program, where the top personnel of the local ball-bearing plant teach production, sales, quality control, and administration to the top personnel of a steel foundry in Rangoon. And the top personnel of Burmese industrial plants come to your community to exchange ideas.

Now the important thing is, *you* do this. Not your president. Not your government. *You* make democracy work the way it must work if it is to survive today's challenges. Any takers? This is "sacrifice."

Another answer to "what went wrong" in the world around us comes from a cab driver in New York City. He told me one day that things went wrong because "the big boys goofed."

That taxi driver did not know that in the United States the line from "little guys" who know little about what goes on in the world, to the "big boys" who "goofed" from China to Cuba, is a direct one. That housewife in Milwaukee did not know that the line from the world where people want change, to her world where she is now asked to face problems of survival, is also a direct one.

When President Kennedy issued his warning he said the self-discipline of the free people had to match the discipline of the mailed fist. The problem he spelled out was: Can we survive the communist challenge?

But there is another problem at least as great. Can this nation survive its housewives, its cab drivers, its business executives, its laborers, and the rest who are uninformed and free to go on being uninformed about the kind of world they live in, people who do not know that in a democracy it is the individual citizen, the "little guy" who sets the example for the "big guys"; that it is he who really decides whether or not policies, foreign or domestic, can work? In other words, can this nation, can freedom, survive free people?

CHAPTER 15

Dirt, People, and History—I

DEATH WEARS MANY FACES. One of the most familiar of its faces today is the mushroom cloud born in the explosive release of energy from the atom. In the summer of 1923, for the crew of a freighter about five hundred miles out to sea, heading toward New York, death wore a roughly similar face in clouds born from the release of a different kind of energy. That energy has been at work in the world throughout history, and has resulted in many times more destruction than could be equaled now by all the nuclear power stored in existing stockpiles of atomic weapons.

The crew of that ship did not know the face of death they saw that day in the clouds that appeared, slowly stretching as far as the eye could see from horizon to horizon. It was a strange sight. It made them uneasy, because the ship's barometer showed nothing wrong. The ship's radio reported no weather warning. The captain decided to take all emergency precautions, then headed into the approaching cloudbank to await the unknown.

The unknown came quickly. It fell out of the sky as soon as the ship moved into the cloud's outer edge, a reddish-brown, gritty stuff, penetrating every nook and cranny of the vessel. They did not recognize it for what it was. It was a sign that somewhere, a nation had begun to die a little. It was an age-old sign. Throughout human history it has spelled the destruction of more nations and peoples than have been destroyed in war.

It began, in this instance, in 1923, during the hot summer months out in the western and midwestern United States, in little whirlwinds called "dust devils." Dust devils are pint-sized cyclones, a few dozen feet high. They have been around the American plains and grasslands for thousands of years. For hundreds of years they were pint-sized annoyances to millions of buffalo and other plains animals that fed on those grasslands. They were a minor annoyance to the Indians. Their tepees and grass-covered summer shelters might go down under an exceptionally strong one, but little more damage was done until late in the Nineteenth Century. Something happened out in the American West then which was to make dust devils and strong prairie winds full-sized annoyances to this nation, and a face of death in clouds like those seen by the crew of the ship at sea many miles away.

The time was April 22, 1889. The place was the borders of what was called the Indian Territory. The Choctaw Indians who lived there had a word for that territory, which in translation meant "Home of the Red Man." That word was "Oklahoma." At two o'clock in the afternoon, twenty thousand Americans broke a solemn treaty with five Indian nations and charged into Oklahoma to carve it into farmland. The event was the Oklahoma Land Rush.

The Oklahoma Land Rush was a special kind of event in American history, because of what happened about a year later. An important incident took place somewhere in that former home of the Red Man. The incident involved a settler who was busily at work one morning soon after the Land Rush trying to clear the grass and sod cover from his new homestead. At one point, he had the uncomfortable feeling that he was being watched. When he looked around he saw on a small ridge a Cherokee Indian watching him in his back-breaking effort to get to the soil underneath to plant his crops. The Indian was not armed. He was alone, and he stood silently watching. The farmer was uneasy, but he saw no reason to expect trouble in the Indian's presence. He turned back to his plow. He soon forgot all about the Indian.

Two hours later he noticed the Indian was still there, still quietly watching. The farmer did not know what to make of this, but he was disturbed enough to walk over to the Indian and ask why he was there. The Indian told him. He raised his arm, pointed to the newly turned grass and sod, spoke three words, and walked off. The farmer watched him go, chuckled, muttered something about ignorant barbarians, and went back to his plowing.

That meeting occurred late in May, 1889. A year later, the farmer had good reason to remember the Indian's words, but not with a chuckle. Dust devils and prairie winds passed over land like his which was no longer protected by grass or sod. It dried the exposed soil, then picked it up and blew it some-place else.

The Indian's three words spoken that day were "wrong side up." He was right. One year after those white-skinned farmers finished turning Oklahoma "wrong side up," Congress declared Oklahoma a "disaster area" and voted emergency aid to help the farmers.

But what those farmers began then has not stopped yet. Nearly every year in states like Oklahoma, which have large areas that do not get enough rainfall to grow much more than grass, there is a crisis in farming or in stock raising. Millions of tax dollars have gone into bailing out Americans who have tried and still try uselessly to turn good grasslands into bad farmlands.

That day in May, 1889, an Indian warned a farmer that grasslands were not farmlands. Thirty-five years later the warning took a deadly but familiar shape during a week of particularly strong west winds. They passed over Oklahoma and blew millions of acres of dried-out, unprotected soil into clouds so dense that they frightened the crew of a freighter five hundred miles at sea.

American land was blowing away. The land had been misused. Reddish-brown dirt from American farms fell out of the sky on that freighter at sea. It was part of the remains of what had been some of the richest land on this planet.

It was the face of death.

Quite a few people who lived in earlier times could have told us this. For example, the people who once lived in the Middle East. They could have warned Americans about this, because they saw that face of death in their own day although they, too, found it hard to recognize.

War is the most popular reason given by historians for the ruin of so many older civilizations which now are represented only by impressive piles of stone. At some point in history, as the historians have it, some stronger people came along to conquer others who lived in those now dead cities of Timgad, Petra, and Babylon. That is an exciting version of history and such things did happen; but it is not the whole story, or even the most important part.

The records left behind by many peoples give no hint that they expected to end up in the junk heap of history. The records show that most of these peoples were proud, sure of their military power, confident that the future would bring them better lives and greater riches. They saw themselves at the peak of their power, even as they stood on the edge of the junk heap of history.

They did not see what was happening around them. What happened, happened to the land under their feet. They misused the land. The land died, and so did one nation after another on those lands. They were weakened from the inside, or rather from the land up.

Plato, the ancient Greek philosopher, tried to explain this to the people of his country not long before Greece gave up its place as one of the greatest civilizations of all time.

"There are mountains in our land now, which can keep nothing but bees," he wrote. "Not so very long ago they were covered by fine timber, to roof the largest buildings. Our country offered boundless pasture for our cattle. Now the rains fall on barren lands and are not stored, but are lost to the sea."

Greek resources, Plato told his people, were gone. Timber had been cut down, but not replaced. The soil was blown or washed away from farms and pasture lands. The mines were worked out.

About twenty-three hundred years later President Kennedy sent a special message to the Congress of the United States which was a modern version of that warning to the ancient Greeks.

"Our entire society rests upon, is dependent upon, our water, our land, our forests and our minerals," Mr. Kennedy told the people. "How we use these resources influences our health, our security, economy, and well-being."

He then warned that Americans are cutting down trees faster than we replace them. Our topsoils are being washed and blown away. Our minerals are being used up at increasing rates.

An ancient Greece, weakened by that process, was replaced a short time later by Rome as the leading nation in the world, to the great surprise of many Greeks who were no better prepared to understand Plato in their day than most of this nation was prepared for the President's warning in February, 1961.

One of the main reasons we are not prepared to understand that message is that we do not see lands dying.

Can "dying lands" explain the bulging warehouses and storage bins that store the surpluses we take from our land? There may indeed be critical shortages of other things, as the President warned, but obviously there is no shortage of food.

Few problems we have faced in our history have received so much publicity during the past few years as our food surplus problems. Most of it has been political talk, election time complaints about how much it costs to store our surpluses. Considerably less has been said about what we are storing. Not all of it is food. Much of the stored material has been cotton, tobacco, and other nonedibles. All of it would be used up quickly if there were to be a few years of the kind of weather that gave us the "dust bowl" of the middle Thirties. We have had that kind of weather quite often in our history, but we have never had one hundred and ninety million Americans to be fed. Actually, we have a year's supply of some surplus items, and little more than a two-year supply of others. Is that truly a "surplus"?

There would be very little concern about our food surplus problem if there were twelve to fifteen million more American mouths to feed right now. We can produce for that many more people right now. That is why we have our surplus headache. But, we add three million more people to our population every year. That means we are about three to five years ahead of our population in the amount we can produce from our land: not really a big margin to play with.

This does not mean that in three to five years there won't be enough food in America for two hundred million Americans. Science and technology have not run out of wonders to perform on American farms. They can make a better future possible for us, provided we do not have to waste our science and technology on the kind of land problems that have led other nations to the junk heap of history. The kind of problem that exists now in the Raft River Valley in Idaho.

The Raft River Valley has been sheep country for sixty years. Around 1900 it ranked with the best winter pasture lands in the nation. Its thick heavy stands of grass had fed and supported a heavy wildlife population for thousands of years. But fifty years after the turn of this century, the Raft River Valley changed. One day a rancher put a flock of eight hundred and seventy-six sheep out to winter pasture. The next day he returned to see another of the many faces of death; this time *on* the land. All his sheep were dead.

Thousands of sheep died in the Raft River Valley that year; and thousands of others died in nine western states where a plant called halogeton was found growing on many parts of the two million acres.

Halogeton is an unusual plant, the only one to be honored by a special act of Congress. In 1952, halogeton was found to be spreading like wildfire around our western states on lands where too many sheep and cattle had been kept too long, killing the grass cover. On that abused land the halogeton grows, beautiful and deadly, because it stores oxalic acid in its leaves and stems. It is a poison. One-half pound of this plant will kill a full-grown sheep. Three pounds of it will kill a full-grown steer. As a result, pasture and range lands covered in part by this plant can feed and fatten less than half as many animals today as they could in 1900. However, in 1900 there were less than half as many Americans demanding lamb chops and beef steaks as there are today.

How did those lands get that way?

Because of the kind of American history that began the day the Pilgrims came ashore in New England. The early colonies in America were originally financed by trading companies that wanted profits from their risky investments. The Plymouth Pilgrims were among the many people in Europe who wanted freedom from political and religious persecution, but their contract with their backers said that for the first seven years they would work to turn profits out of the new American land. They had no great concern about what happened to the land in the process of working off that debt.

This is not the kind of history we get in our history books, but it is American history, and it explains a really incredible record of land abuse for over three hundred years.

When the first colonist from the Old World set foot on North America in the 1600s there was enough soil covering the surface of what are now the United States to make an even layer nine inches deep across the continent. Keep in mind the fact that it takes about seven thousand years of geological and biological action to turn out one inch of that soil. That nine-inch layer represented about sixty-five thousand years of soil development.

Since men began to farm, graze, and deforest America in the early 1600s, one-third of that original nine inches is gone, destroyed by misuse and abuse. In three hundred years, Americans managed to destroy as much soil as had been laid down in North America in about twenty thousand years. Most of that land loss came from five hundred million acres that were originally good for farming at no great expense.

One hundred million acres were destroyed by men like that farmer in Oklahoma after the Land Rush in 1889. Another hundred million acres were so damaged by men like those ranchers in Idaho as to make the growth of halogeton possible.

As President Kennedy put this same matter to Congress in February, 1961, too much of our soil is still being washed and blown away. The process began with colonists and settlers like the Pilgrims (who first wanted to go to Guinea, where they hoped to find gold and easy riches) and colonists like John Winthrop, Governor of Massachusetts, who came to America to regain the wealth and social position he had lost at home.

What began with many of the early colonists who saw the New World as a quick step to fame and easy riches has been carried on by their descendants. In the State of Washington not long ago, one of those descendants, a lumberman, objected to a law which said that he had to put in seedlings to replace every tree he cut down. The lumberman objected on two grounds. First, he said, the land belonged to him and no one had the right to tell him what to do with it. That law, he said, was a violation of his right to hold and enjoy private property. His second objection was that reseeding and restocking his land denied him a reasonable profit from lumbering.

The lumberman's case went to the United States Supreme Court in 1950. It marked an important turning point in American history, as was made clear by the title of the decision handed down: it was called *A Pact with the Unborn.*

That lumber operator, said the court, had the responsibility to see that future generations of Americans would also be able to benefit from the use of the land. His interests and rights were no longer the only matters involved. The nation's future was involved. In Ancient Greece, Plato spelled out the same problem for the people of his country. The Supreme Court spelled it out for Americans of the Twentieth Century.

That Supreme Court decision in 1950, and the Halogeton Act passed by Congress in 1952, put American dollars and our science and technology to work, not to make America richer and stronger, but to keep America from becoming poorer and weaker. It is vitally important for us to realize that this is not the historical road America has traveled in the past to become a rich and powerful leader of nations.

On some of the richest lands to be found anywhere on this planet, using some of the richest, highest quality resources on earth, we built this nation. In the beginning the cost was low to use our lands, and the profits were high. The difference between those low costs and high profits has always added up to our high standard of living. But the Halogeton Act was one of the new facts which has been eating into those profits. No nation ever became wealthy, or remained powerful, by frittering away its profits to correct the mistakes made by irresponsible men. That was why the Supreme Court decision of 1950 was an important turning point in American history. It served notice that this nation cannot afford any more irresponsible men. This is important, not because our high living standards are at stake, or our power, or our ideas about justice. It is important because our kind of freedom is at stake.

That kind of freedom grew among a people with elbowroom; few Americans in a big land. With plenty of elbowroom, twenty-three million Americans back in 1889 were free to turn their Oklahomas upside down irresponsibly; and they didn't mind too much when the United States government stepped in to help them. Today's much larger American population has less of that "elbowroom," on farmlands, in mines, in good water, good air, or in any natural resource. Today's American has less, and poorer quality resources to work and live with. We are no longer free to do as we please with them; but many among us today still mind very much that, since stepping in to help deal with problems like that emergency in 1890, the government has never really stepped out of what were once our private affairs.

This resentment has led to a new parlor game in this country during the last thirty years, a dangerous game of name-calling called "creeping socialism." It is played by too many Americans today who simplify things too much. Often they know little or nothing about the kind of American history made by irresponsible men who forced the government into what were then our private affairs. That record clearly shows what happens when individual Americans misuse their private affairs by making them public problems. When that point is reached, the government always steps in.

Americans who play this dangerous new game of "creeping

socialism" see that government, their government, as one of the greatest dangers to our future as a free people. In doing so they misuse the word "socialism" and they misread their own history. The problem has never been "creeping socialism" in our American government. It has always been creeping irresponsibility among too many Americans.

CHAPTER 16

Dirt, People, and History—II

ONE OF THE DEADLIEST KILLERS in human history recently took the lives of more than twenty-six thousand Americans in one year. No one really knows how or why it does its deadly work in the bodies of men and animals. All that is known about it is that up to a point it is a normal living cell. Suddenly, it goes "wild." In that condition, it kills.

Medical and health laboratories all over the world have been hard at work for years, trying to discover what triggers normal cells to become wild cells. In an American laboratory recently, an experiment was carried out which suggested some possible answers. In that experiment, dirt taken out of the air we breathe in cities and towns was blown into the lungs of several laboratory animals. That dirt apparently had some special properties which did not appear until it entered the animal's lungs. Once in its lungs, something in that dirt triggered normal cells to become wild ones.

192

After separating the different materials in a sample of that air-borne dirt, one item was isolated which proved to be the "trigger" in that experiment. It was a substance called benzopyrene, very important in our lives today. The kind of world we live in today would be impossible without it. But that experiment in a medical laboratory in California suggested one reason at least why people around the world, in cities like Los Angeles, have found life to be nearly impossible with benzopyrene.

That fact had its start in an incident that took place in October, 1542, when a Spaniard named Juan Rodriguez Cabrillo sailed into a small bay on the southern coast of what is California today. Captain Cabrillo noticed something peculiar about the place, and he wrote it into his diary.

> The tops of the mountains can be seen clearly despite the great distance. But their bases cannot be seen because of the heavy layer of smoke from the Indian fires. The smoke rises almost straight up, then spreads out at a certain point to cover the entire valley.

Captain Cabrillo named that place the "Bay of Smokes." Then he sailed off to explore other places.

Four hundred years later another incident took place in the Bay of Smokes. This second incident created a stir in what was then the Army Air Corps, because a particular cloud layer was over the bay area, but it was not supposed to be where it was. The clouds hung more or less at that point above the ground where Captain Cabrillo, in his time, had seen a heavy smoke layer covering the valley.

In 1942, the area was dotted by air bases. These clouds created a stir because at that point in World War II there was no effective ground control system to bring pilots and planes down if they were in trouble. Many pilots trying to land planes found themselves in trouble along the California coast because of clouds and fog. For some reason, the weather forecasters could not predict cloud formations in that region.

For some reason, the rules of forecasting did not work in Captain Cabrillo's Bay of Smokes.

Why not?

This problem, after a number of crashes, became the basis for a major research project. It was known that there were other places in the world where the same problem existed; places Americans expected to send pilots and planes during World War II.

That research project turned up some interesting kinds of dirt in the air around today's city of Los Angeles. That dirt had certain properties, which made it possible for clouds to form when they were not supposed to, according to the rules of forecasting. That dirt changed many rules, and extended beyond the lives of wartime pilots. Since then, what has been learned about the properties of the air above many parts of this nation has changed the rules of living for millions of Americans.

In Washington, D. C., for example, a housewife took down some dirty curtains one day, tossed them into a washing machine, poured in some soap, and then watched some of her rules of living change.

Her curtains disintegrated into bits and pieces.

For the same reason, in Los Angeles in the late Forties, women were irritated when their blouses, skirts, and stockings, made of certain synthetic materials, disintegrated and fell off in bits and pieces, sometimes in public gathering places.

This phenomenon was no more painful to the ladies of Los Angeles than to a number of house owners in Reading, Ohio. They discovered one morning that their houses had changed color during the night. The previous day their houses had been painted all kinds of colors, but on that morning, all the houses turned black. A farmer in Los Angeles also was reported to be having color trouble at that same time; his hens laid green eggs.

In those and other places such things happened because an

American city like Los Angeles pours as much as eight thous-
and tons of dirt, fumes and other waste material into its air
each day from automobiles alone. Factories, home heating
units, incinerators, and other fires will add thousands of additional tons of debris every day. About a thousand tons of the
total are made up of hydrocarbons like benzopyrene. Time
after time that substance has triggered wild cells—cancer cells
—in laboratory animals. That garbage in the air has given
cities around the world sewers in their skies.

The key to what happened to those curtains in Washington,
D. C.; those clothes in Los Angeles; the paint on those houses
in Ohio; and those eggs in California is in that aerial garbage.
It is a vitally important key to a world in which increasing
numbers of people, plants and animals cannot live.

Any high school student in a chemistry class can duplicate
that kind of world through simple, controlled experiments in
a test tube. Mix several chemicals thoroughly and heat them
under pressure, exposing the tube to different concentrations
of light and moisture. Then cool them, or in any way change
the conditions affecting that chemical mixture. The result will
be a wide variety of chemical reactions.

Now, think of that air as a test tube over the one hundred
and ninety-two metropolitan areas in this country; New York,
Chicago, Los Angeles, and so on. Into that test tube, every
day, thousands of tons of chemicals are dumped from automobile exhausts, factories and homes. Imagine them mixed
thoroughly in that test tube, heated by the sun, affected by
changing air pressures and moisture. Then imagine what kind
of reactions go on in that air mass that we breathe.

You will have to imagine practically all of it, because very
little is known about what goes on there, except that under
certain conditions, curtains and clothes disintegrate, chemicals
in the air work on chemicals in those fabrics, on lead-based
paints, on the feed for chickens.

There was clear warning for us in an incident in October,

1948, in Donora, Pennsylvania, that the garbage poured into our air each day could do more than that. That garbage breathed into human lungs could kill too.

For four days that October, chemical wastes from Donora's industries were mixed in a fog bank that settled over the town and did not move. Just what happened is not known. The sulfur dioxide in that air could have been responsible. So could the hydrochloric acid, or the carbon monoxide, or any one of the thirty other chemicals known to be in the air over practically all our industrial areas today. Whatever it was, in four days, twenty people died of poisonous fumes in Donora.

Any one of those chemicals would be deadly. But what happens when they are taken together?

Taken together in London, in 1952, they killed four thousand people in six days; six days of much the same kind of fog and smog that hit Donora a few years earlier.

In the month following that London incident, eight thousand more deaths were traced to what was described as smog poisoning.

These were not the first such incidents. In December, 1930, in the industrial valley of the Meuse in Belgium, the shape of things to come in America and England had been seen in a fog full of chemical garbage that killed sixty-three people. There have been other incidents. There will be more.

You breathe sixteen thousand quarts of air every day, air filled with the same kind of dirt. Day after day such dirt causes cells to go wild in human bodies. Dr. Hueper of the United States National Cancer Institute has stated that dirt in the air was one of the big reasons for the growing number of lung cancer cases in America. Dr. Leroy Burney, President Eisenhower's surgeon general of the nation, said stomach cells could go wild when affected by the dirt we swallow from the air, not just by breathing it.

The truth is that our world has become less livable as it has become more industrial. This is a little known fact a long way

removed from the comfortable, popularly accepted view of the
kind of future we're headed for, and of what tomorrow's world
is supposed to be.

For four years a special committee of the American Association for the Advancement of Science worked on a report for
its two million members, a report that did not make headlines
despite its really enormous importance.

That report said the nation had reached the point where
scientists had to speak up about the cost of what we have been
calling progress. The nation could no longer afford to put
twelve and one-half billion dollars every year into developing
new and more things; and only ten to fifteen million dollars
a year into finding ways of getting rid of new and more waste,
like the chemical garbage being dumped into the air. That report said these United States had reached another turning
point in American history, where thirty chemicals in our air
were changing our future.

What that means can be made clear by a simple glass of
water, the kind more and more of us get from the water
faucets in our homes every day.

Few Americans worry about the quality of the water in their
homes today. It has been a long time since we had to worry
about good drinking water. It has been taken for granted that
modern scientific methods for purifying water have licked all
the water problems, except perhaps the problem of enough
water.

What is there to worry about where good, pure water is
concerned?

What there is to worry about can be seen in filter basins of
sewage disposal plants across the nation today. Those basins
are covered with a foamy substance that frequently climbs to
heights of fifteen feet and more; a sight seen for the first time
shortly after the end of World War II. Since then, public
health people have been increasingly concerned, because in
more and more places there is a direct connection between

foam in a sewage disposal plant and foam in drinking water. The chemical waste, the garbage in those sewage plants, is getting into more and more water supplies; and in those places, drinking water is no longer pure.

This is because there is a vast difference between two chemical compounds found in practically any American home today: soap and detergent. Before World War II, soap was by far the most widely used cleaning agent in the nation. In 1939, America used over three billion pounds of it, dumping it into septic tanks, sewage disposal plants, or directly into rivers and streams after use. In these places bacteria, or filter beds, or chemicals would break down the soap, and so get rid of that chemical compound.

Today, in place of soap, we use about four billion pounds of detergent which we also dump into septic tanks, sewage disposal systems, and directly into rivers and streams. But there the similarity ends. Detergent is not broken down by bacteria. It is not filtered out by anything. Chemicals do not get rid of it.

Detergent seeps right through those controls, unchanged, and is picked up again by cities and towns using river or ground water. For those places, detergents have become a serious problem. Very little is known about the effect of the detergent materials on the human body. A great deal of money has gone into the development of this soap substitute, but very little has been spent studying ways to get rid of it, or its effects on living things.

This chemical compound is one symbol of the turning point in American history that was touched on by the report of the Association for the Advancement of Science. That was a turning point that moved us into a world where there are, today, about five hundred thousand chemical compounds. Now, this statistic may not mean much to you, until you realize that before World War II there were only a few hundred such compounds. For twenty years the twelve and one-half billion dollars we spend annually on research has turned out thousands of new compounds every year. All of these must be disposed of somehow, somewhere.

Practically all those compounds end up in the nation's rivers and streams, or off our shores at sea. In those places we now have the same sewer problem that we have in the air. This has been made very clear in places like the Ohio River, where recently some strange material was discovered.

That material did not come from any of the sewage systems emptying into the Ohio. It is not the result of anything that grew in the river under natural conditions. It has appeared there since a growing number of industries started using Ohio River water after the end of World War II.

Placed under a microscope, some of the new material is found heavily loaded with disease organisms; and that simply intensifies the mystery. What is this stuff? Where did it come from?

One possible answer to this question was given in testimony before the Committee on Appropriations in the House of Representatives. One of the witnesses testifying on the use of rivers and streams as chemical dumping grounds told about an incident in Alabama a few years ago.

A plant located on a river hired a testing laboratory to find out whether or not wastes from a pesticide they were about to produce could be dumped into that river for disposal.

The testing company found that the chemicals involved were the kind that bacteria in the river could break down. Permission was given to put that company's wastes in the river.

Soon after, a textile plant moved in to use the same river to get rid of its dyes. The same testing company checked those dyes, found them to be the kind that would break down properly in the river, and the state gave the permission to dump these wastes in the river.

A third industry moved in. The same routine was followed. It too was given permission to use the river as a sewer.

Each of those chemical waste items tested out safely. But when they were mixed together unexpected things happened. Chemical reactions led to foul smells; people in towns along the river became ill. Expensive emergency measures had to be taken because not enough was known about this problem of mixing new wastes, and no one had really cared enough to do anything before an emergency developed.

Another emergency occurred in Washington, D. C., a few years ago, in an outbreak of infectious hepatitis among children in nearby Prince George County, Maryland.

This disease is hard to fight, and it is very contagious. It also has one interesting characteristic; it is caused by a virus that gets around in certain kinds of polluted water. The same kind of dirty water that gave bacillary dysentery to fourteen hundred people in one upstate New York town. Polluted water reached those people through the water faucets in their homes.

An epidemic of typhoid fever was reported to have started in the same way in upper New Hampshire early in 1960; and similar emergencies were reported that year in the Congressional Committee on Appropriations hearings of 1960.

All these situations developed in places where for years people have taken it for granted that water from any public water supply must be pure water, and was not to be questioned.

The people of Atchison, Kansas, became worried about their public water supply a few years ago. They use the Missouri River, twenty-four miles downstream from St. Joseph, Missouri.

The people of St. Joseph have dumped their raw sewage into the Missouri River for over a hundred years. What eighty thousand of them dumped there in our time was only a part of the problem affecting Atchison's water supply. In that water were tons of chemicals that had been washed off farmlands for hundreds of miles upstream, chemicals from fertilizers and insecticides. To use that water Atchison had to add so many

neutralizing chemicals that eventually people were made sick
by drinking the loaded stuff.

In September, 1960, that emergency situation in a twenty-
four-mile stretch of the Missouri River became another important turning point in American history.

For the first time in American history, the United States
government went to court to force an American community
to do something it did not want to do.

St. Joseph did not want to put in a sewage disposal plant.
Twice in three years the citizens of that city had voted against
building a sewage plant.

For those people, and for the nation, the word "freedom"
changed meaning in September, 1960. Americans learned they
were no longer free to behave irresponsibly in ways that would
endanger the health of their neighbors.

In the same way, in Philadelphia, Pennsylvania, other Americans discovered that a man's home was no longer his castle.
In 1959, a public health inspector walked into a private apartment to check on possible dangers to the health of the community. The inspector had no warrant. Therefore he had no
right to invade the traditional privacy of the American home,
said the people who took the case to court.

They lost that case.

The decision handed down by the court said, in effect, that
private rights could no longer be considered more important
than the public welfare.

These were two important court cases which served notice
that the nation could no longer afford irresponsible actions by
individuals that endangered the public welfare.

America's high standard of living is at stake in the worsening
problems of dirty air and dirty water. Power and justice are
at stake too. But, more important, our freedom is at stake.

With elbowroom, Americans have been fairly free to dump
their garbage into their air and water. But one hundred and
ninety million Americans no longer have this freedom. That

freedom has now become license—a threat to the nation's future.

The future we shall know is a matter economists have been haggling about in trying to determine how much economic growth is needed to keep us a leading world power. Shall we grow at a rate of 3 per cent a year, 5 per cent, 8 per cent or what per cent? They argue as though all that is needed is a decision.

That may have been possible for an America that had no need to worry about its resources, resources like good water and good air to support tomorrow's economic growth. But we have a resource problem now.

They do not have to be insurmountable problems. We know how to control air and water pollution. Ten billion dollars spent on new sewage disposal plants in places like St. Joseph, Missouri, would remove pollution from nearly all the nation's water. The same amount would solve our air pollution problems.

The problem is not money. It is a problem of education, education to inform Americans about the close tie that has always existed between a wide margin of resources and freedom. Reduce that margin of resources, reduce the quality of those resources, and you reduce what Americans have always meant by the word "freedom."

CHAPTER 17

Bombs, Babies, and Biology—I

ONE OF THE MOST IMPORTANT battles in history took place
in the Thirteenth Century in a place called Liegnitz, Poland.
Just what happened there isn't known exactly. European history
books written in Europe after that event say that an invasion
force of Mongols and Russians was stopped there by a defending force of Poles, Czechs, and Germans. But history books
written in China at the same time disagree. The Chinese say
that after that battle there were no Poles, Czechs, or Germans
around to stop anybody. That Mongol-led invasion force, under
a man named Temuchin, wiped them out at Liegnitz, the
westernmost point reached by the armies that started out
twenty-five years earlier to conquer the world.

To conquer and dominate the world has been the dream
and aim of some men at every stage in history. No man came
closer to realizing that dream than Temuchin. The Emperor
of Heaven, the Mongols called him. The rest of the world to
this day knows him as Genghis Khan.

Temuchin started an empire that reached from the Pacific Ocean in the east to Poland. It encompassed most of present-day Russia, and sizable chunks of Southeast Asia, and the Middle East. There had been nothing to compare with such an empire before his time. There has been nothing to match it since.

Other men have matched the Great Khan in aim, however. Today his aims are surpassed by the men who rule communist China, which reaches into what was once the heartland of Genghis Khan. These rulers of China are as confident as the Great Khan ever was that the world can be dominated by a single state. Like Temuchin, they have weapons to support their aims. Unlike Temuchin, their most powerful weapon is not military, although it can be used as effectively to change the world.

Communist China's most powerful weapon today is a statistic. It shows that most of the children born in the world every day are Chinese; one of every four. The next largest group is born in India; one of every eight. A long way down that list are American and Russian babies. One of every twenty is Russian. One of every twenty-three is American.

It is very important for us to know that Americans and Russians are low on that list because, despite their size, not many people, comparatively speaking, live in either Russia or America; despite the importance of both nations in world affairs today. A large part of the reason for the importance of America and Russia in the world today is due to the fact that there are not many people in either place. For their size, America and Russia are among the least populated places on earth, and thus, they are unusual places.

Both nations are rich in their own territory: in coal, oil, copper, lead, and the other resources that a nation must have to be a power in today's world.

Babies born in those two countries are born rich in raw materials, and rich in the kind of history that made it possible for Americans and Russians to become what they are today.

This is not true for most of the two hundred and eighty thousand infants born into the world each day. An Indian infant, for example, comes into the world on a land base about half the size of the United States, with a population more than twice as large, around four hundred and thirty million people. At birth the American youngster has fifteen thousand tons of coal as his share of that raw material in the United States. At birth an Indian youngster has two hundred tons of coal as his share of the coal in India.

That example for coal holds true for practically everything else. There is less of everything in India, and now that country is trying to build the Twentieth Century version of the good life, which is based on things like coal, while adding eight million people to its population every year.

Indians want that good life. Most of them have been working hard for it. But for most of them it comes hard, and slowly, if at all. This has been the case in India for an important and now dangerous reason.

It is important and dangerous in more and more places. Consider Java, in the Republic of Indonesia. A Javanese youngster is born on an island about the size of our Alabama or Iowa. The population in Alabama is around three million today, but that Javanese youngster is born with fifty-six million neighbors.

What do you suppose life would be like in Alabama, or Iowa, if fifty-six million people lived in those places, instead of three million; and a million people were to be added every year?

Population pressure alone explains why the Twentieth Century version of the good life has been so slow in coming for people like the Javanese, and the Egyptians, and the Ceylonese, and our own Puerto Ricans, and the Pakistanis, and the Chinese.

In all those places the good life has not come rushing in; and this was predicted over one hundred and fifty years ago by a man who described what he considered the most important problem affecting the future of the human race. What that man wrote about in 1798 has in fact become one of the most explosive sets of political and economic facts of the Sixties, for a simple and powerful reason that has been made clear in many a high school biology class through another controlled test tube experiment.

In that experiment a test tube is filled with bacteria. Another tube is filled with a liquid food solution. A microscope is used to count the number of bacteria in a sample taken from the test tube, and then a certain amount of food is added every twenty minutes. What happens is crystal clear. After twenty minutes, the number of bacteria in that tube has doubled. As the same amount of food is added every twenty minutes, the number of bacteria continues to double. It is a simple little mathematical formula that bears heavily on many of our problems at home and abroad today. That formula looks like this:

A   1 — 2 — 3 — 4 — 5 — 6 — 7 — 8 — 9
B   1 — 2 — 4 — 8 — 16 — 32 — 64 — 128 — 256

Line A represents the number of drops of food added to the test tube containing the bacteria. Line B represents the number of times the bacteria multiplied every time food was added. The important thing is that the rate of multiplication for the bacteria was many times greater than the rate at which food was made available to them. The difference between those two series of numbers has become political and economic dynamite in our time. You see, that difference does not last. At some point, the speed with which the bacteria increase slows down. There are too many of them for the amount of food available. With no food surplus, they begin to compete for food. They fight for it. Fewer and fewer bacteria are born; more die of hunger. The number of bacteria in that tube then levels off, at the point where there is just enough food to keep that test tube population alive. A balance is reached at the edge of starvation. The same number of bacteria are born as die. There is no further increase in the population.

That example with bacteria is a laboratory version of what, in 1798, the Reverend Thomas Robert Malthus said goes on among human beings too.

Human population grows faster than the food supply. As in the test tube, a balance is reached. The population gets just enough to stay alive. To help keep the balance, starvation, war, and disease keep the number of human deaths about even with the number of human births. Exactly the way it was with the bacteria in the test tube.

Malthus saw the population problem, or the population explosion, as we call it today, as the most dangerous problem affecting the future of the human race.

His was not a happy book. It has been the cause of constant argument since it was written. Few written works have ever caused such a furor.

And nowhere has Malthus caused more controversy than among the rulers of communist Russia.

As every good Marxist and communist believes, there is no such thing as overpopulation: that is, too many people to be supported by their economy. There can never be too many people. It is all a matter of increasing production.

As every good communist knows, labor is the real source of values. Labor, not capital, produces wealth. People make things; money does not. To have more things, to produce more things, to buy more things, to make more wealth: Produce more people.

The greater the number of customers, the greater production must be, and in this way the economy grows, producing the things people need at a faster rate than population grows.

This is a basic Marxist belief. No one can get angrier than a Marxist or a communist at the suggestion that perhaps Malthus was right. That is, in a communist Russia. In a communist

China there has been an interesting difference of opinion about this matter.

A few years ago Mao Tse-tung made it clear that he thought Malthus may not have been wrong about overpopulation, under certain conditions. Out of that incident came the weapon that can lead to the destruction of nations, and help strongly to remake the world in the Chinese communist image.

In the mid-1950s some peculiar reports began to come out of communist China, about unemployment in many of that country's industrial cities and towns. At the same time, a "back to the village" program was set up across that nation to cut down on what the Chinese communists described as too many newcomers to the cities and towns. The people were to go back to the farms they came from.

That was also the time when China made what has been called the "Great Leap Forward." Five hundred and fifty million farming people went into twenty-six thousand communes.

It was described as a new way of life. Nothing like this change had ever happened so quickly before, to any sizeable group of people.

Suddenly, without warning, these things were emphasized in the middle 1950s. Communist China's policies at home changed. It was obvious that something was happening, but what? And why?

It simply is not normal for a Marxist or a communist to admit that unemployment is possible under communism. When Mr. Khrushchev made his tour of the United States in 1959, he said that unemployment was always a capitalist problem, never a communist one. But communist China admitted it had that problem.

How come?

Why did Mao order people back to the villages?

In our history, when we changed America from a farming to an industrial nation, we never had to worry about too many newcomers to our cities and towns. As a matter of fact we sent agents to Europe and Asia to hire as much foreign labor as they could find. We could not get our farmers out of our villages and off our farms into our factories fast enough.

But China is different. The main reason is that as recently as 1955 about half the children in China died before they were five years old. Public health programs were started in China in 1950 to change that. Today it *has been changed.* About sixty thousand youngsters born in that country every day means that an average of eighteen million people are added to China's population every year. The fact is, China's population is growing faster than its economy can meet the needs of eighteen million new mouths to feed, bodies to clothe and house and put to work every year. This does not mean the Chinese economy is not growing. It is, at a faster rate than ours; but not fast enough to give eighteen million new pairs of hands industrial jobs. Mao knew idle hands are dangerous, so he sent them out of the cities, back to the villages; but not to loaf and complain there, and perhaps revolt against the state. The idea was to have the Chinese peasantry work under strict supervision on the newly established communes, which strengthened the government's control over its people.

The important point in what happened was that communist China is not communist Russia. Nikita Khrushchev may believe that there is no such thing as overpopulation, living as he does in an underpopulated country.

Mao Tse-tung knows better. He lives in an overpopulated country. In 1956 he put into effect in China one of the most drastic birth control programs ever undertaken by any nation. He wanted time to build up his economy by holding back population growth.

He did not get it. The program was a failure. China's public health program cut down the death rate, while Chinese parents continued to do what came naturally. China's population skyrocketed. At that point Mao Tse-tung made what may turn out to be China's most important decision in its drive to be the leading world power. He abandoned the effort to control population growth, and attempted to turn it to advantage.

Mao's decision is important because it is supported by a chemical substance—DDT. What has been done with that pesticide gives Malthus' old ideas new meaning in the new world surrounding postwar Europe and America.

It is the kind of new meaning that grew out of an incident that took place in British Guiana, on the north central coast of South America, one day in 1945. On that day, two health officers from the West Indies visited Guiana's capital, Georgetown. They noticed several funeral processions making their way down the city's main street. The size of the coffins suggested children and so the officer asked about a possible epidemic that might have hit the native population.

The resident health officer said the scene was normal for that time of year. The death rate in Guiana then was three hundred and fifty babies out of every one thousand. To get the significance of that, we must realize that the average in Europe and America is less than thirty per thousand.

That death rate in Guiana shocked those two health officers. They wanted to know what diseases were responsible. The resident health officer told them: insect-carried diseases. Full of horrified sympathy, the health officers suggested using DDT to control the insects.

The prospect of controlling the insects moved the resident health officer to immediate action. As soon as the insecticide was flown in, it was carried to the worst, most infested places. Fields, and swamps, and towns were dusted and sprayed. Soon after this the death rate dropped from three hundred and fifty per thousand births, to sixty-seven per thousand. The health of the native population improved. Parents lived longer. A humanitarian effort was completed.

It paid off in starvation.

Before that DDT changed things in Guiana, the native economy produced just enough to keep the native population alive. With the population explosion that followed the use of that insecticide, the native economy could not do the job.

What disease no longer did, hunger began to do. The death rate began to climb again, and it led directly to a critical change in the politics of Guiana. A change that saw local communists secure a foothold in that country because of the dissatisfaction of its hungry people.

Cheddi Jagan, at the head of the Peoples Progressive Party, almost organized a communist government in British Guiana after the 1957 elections. His party won most of the seats in that country's parliament. It was a massive demonstration of the native population's discontent with things as they were. As things were, and still are in Guiana, they are also in most of the rest of the world. Disease control programs have produced population explosions that are at the heart of practically every problem we face in the world.

The same population problem that thrust a Cheddi Jagan into power in Guiana put a Nasser into power in Egypt and a "guided democracy" into being in Indonesia.

All these developments are not at all what we hoped for since 1945. They are very close to the kind of developments a Mao Tse-tung wants in order to lead his country to world leadership.

This has much to do with Mao Tse-tung's decision late in 1957 to turn the world's growing population problems into victory for his kind of communism.

China's influence in the world will be enormous in less than twenty years if only for one reason. In less than twenty years, given its present population growth, there will be *one billion* Chinese. At that rate, half the human race may be Chinese in less than sixty years. They cannot all live on the China mainland, which is not much larger than the territory of the fifty United States. The Chinese people are going to need living space, just as the Imperial Japanese once needed it, just as the Nazis once needed it, and Mussolini's Italy once needed it.

No nation has done more, for good humanitarian reasons, to wipe out disease in the world than the United States. But in tackling the problem of disease control, we have tackled only a part of the problem.

We have saved many lives, but once saved, what are the Guianians, Egyptians, Indonesians, Javanese, Ceylonese, Pakistanis, Bolivians, and Hottentots to do with their lives? Our answer until now has been that it is not our responsibility. We have no right to interfere in the internal affairs of nations, we said, after spraying our DDT all over the internal affairs of many nations.

The fact is we have no choice but to interfere in the internal affairs of nations, in working with others to prove that communism does not offer the only answers to their problems. We must do this because freedom at home depends heavily on a certain kind of world environment around us. A non-communist world.

CHAPTER 18

Bombs, Babies, and Biology—II

THE EFFECTS OF THE BATTLE at Liegnitz, Poland, mentioned in the preceding chapter, are still felt in Europe, well over seven hundred years later. That fact is a tribute of sorts to the *ordu* of Mongols who planned that invasion of Europe. They were masters of psychological warfare and most other kinds of warfare too. They won that battle in large part because a legend had gone ahead of their armies. The story was that the *ordu* of Mongols that headed west was so large no force could hope to stand against it. When they rode out of the Hungarian plain, that summer morning in the year 1241, they tackled a thoroughly frightened army of Europeans. The Poles, Czechs, and Germans in that defending army were frightened by a single word, "horde."

Europe's troubles in that year 1241 were caused by an invading *ordu* of Mongols. They mispronounced the word then, by calling it "horde" instead of *ordu,* and gave it a different meaning. That meaning is particularly important to people who live in Europe today, because it applies to them now as it never did to the Mongols. The word *ordu* meant a military encampment of a few hundred horsemen. The word horde meant a vast mass of people, in keeping with the legend that moved ahead of the Mongol armies. Mongolia was never a place overrun by hordes of men, but Europe is that kind of place today.

We have used the word horde for years to describe places like Asia, with its masses of Indians, the crowding masses of Chinese, Javanese, Japanese, and Ceylonese. But no place on earth can be described better by that word than today's Europe. It is just as heavily populated as China or India. That fact is at the heart of the drastic changes that have taken place there since the end of World War II; changes that have started to affect our lives too.

Probably the most important of those changes began in Britain in 1945. In the election held that year, most of the British people declared themselves for the Labour Party. This fact left the American public shocked and confused. Winston Churchill's party, and all it stood for, was voted out of office, while the Labour Party, and all it stood for, was voted in. As Americans saw the British elections that year, the issues were simple and clear. We were in the last stages of winning a very costly war. The main job was to get back to building and living the good life as we had been doing before we were rudely interrupted by World War II. Winston Churchill's party was for that too.

Why, then, did the British people vote to put the Labour Party in power when what it stood for was not a return to the good old days, but to a different kind of day in which the government would take over and run Britain's railroads, mines, and public utilities?

That was socialism, as we saw it. Was that what most Britons had fought for in World War II? Did they not want to get

back to the old life? Why did they go socialist? Americans
were convinced that things were not quite right in the Britain
of 1945.

For several important reasons that bear hard on our future,
Americans had better get straight just what happened in Brit-
ain after World War II. That country did not go socialist. The
British would have liked nothing better than to get back to
things as they had been in the days before World War II.
The point is, they could not.

Something had happened to that country which convinced
most British voters by the end of the war that there could be
no return to things as they were. It began before the First
World War bled that nation of its manpower and wealth, and
the empire began to change.

The statistics show what two world wars cost Great Britain
in manpower, but it is harder to measure the cost of war in
iron and steel used or blown up, in tanks and battleships, or
the cost of war in aluminum, and brass and tin and lead destroyed as planes or exploded as shells—instead of being used
in telephones, radios, and can openers to spell the good life in
peace.

The cost of two world wars, the change, the loss of an
empire left the British with very different ideas about the
future than Americans had in 1945. Before World War I, Great
Britain was, with its empire, one of the richest nations in history. Britain was resource-rich in food, and raw materials,
which Englishmen could get easily and cheaply from the empire.

By 1945, those days were over. No economic system in history was freer than Britain's when there was more than enough
wealth to go around. But when there was not enough to go
around, they voted for a planned economy in 1945. A planned
economy, not socialism.

Most Britons were not interested in socialism, but they were
interested in finding ways to hold on to one of the highest

standards of living on earth. With the old empire and its great wealth going or gone by 1945, they saw a planned economy as the best way to keep the highest possible living standards for the greatest number of Englishmen. This meant planning the best use of the wealth that remained, now that the empire was gone. This meant rationing food to give everyone a fair share. Half of Britain's food, it should not be forgotten, must be imported. As much as 90 per cent of Britain's raw materials must be imported. This meant allocating raw materials so that every industry would get a fair share. Most important of all, this meant planning for freedom, to assure every Briton the greatest measure of freedom possible under the conditions Great Britain faced in 1945.

Of all the revolutionary changes that have come about in Britain, none are harder for Americans to understand than that last fact, about planning for freedom. At the heart of what we have always meant by the word is freedom from restriction, freedom from an ordered way of doing things. But planning means restriction. It means an ordered way of doing things. How then can the British, or anyone else, plan freedom? The two words simply do not go together.

We are still where the British were before World War II. What we have always meant by freedom is the kind that is possible where there are enough resources to meet the growing needs of growing numbers of people. Where there is not enough to go around to meet those needs our freedom is not possible.

This fact was made quite clear to a man who started building houses in a town near my home a few years ago. At that time he brought a problem into my office at Yale University.

This man's problem began soon after he sold his twenty-third house, on a one-hundred-acre tract of land he was developing. He wanted to build about a hundred and twenty-five more houses.

Originally those hundred acres had been two farms. It was level land, easy to develop. He had expected no problems, and had faced none—until that twenty-third house was sold. Then he began to get complaints from the people who had moved into his houses about the periods during the day when there was not any water in their plumbing systems.

This water shortage would appear when Mrs. Jones, and Mrs. Brown, and Mrs. Smith, and a number of other housewives, started to do the daily wash; or on warm summer evenings when Mr. Jones, and Mr. Brown, and Mr. Smith, and a number of other husbands, started to water their lawns. The builder's customers were angry. He was baffled. He checked with the two farmers who owned the land before he bought it. They assured him they never had any water problems. He had done everything by the rules in providing water for each house. A six-inch cased well served every building. Each well was serviced by one of the best pumps on the market.

What in the world was wrong?

Because water problems were one of my main interests, he came to me for help. What was wrong for a housing contractor and twenty-three homeowners in that Connecticut town had been wrong for forty-seven million Britons at the end of World War II. On that tract of land, seventy-three Americans moved from the point where there was enough water wealth to go around, to the point where there was not enough wealth to go around. At that point they found that their freedom was affected. They were no longer free to wash their clothes when they wanted to, to water their lawns when they wanted to, cook their meals when they wanted to. They discovered that where there was not enough water, their freedom to use it was restricted. They had to plan its proper use to benefit everyone in that housing development.

That contractor did not understand the difference numbers of people can make. Two families living in two farmhouses on those hundred acres had no water problems. They were re-source-rich. There was more water than they needed. They were free, as we know the word.

Twenty-three families drawing water from twenty-three wells, spaced about one hundred and fifty feet apart on that same land, had water problems. They were resource-poor. There was less water than they needed. They were not free, in exactly the same way that most of the world is not free today. Most of the world is resource-poor.

We solved the contractor's problem by planning; by the proper spacing of those wells, after we figured out how much usable, available water there was under those hundred acres. We figured out how many people could live on that land, using dishwashers, washing machines, garbage disposals, shower baths, and air conditioners. Then, to insure their freedom to enjoy that good life, the contractor built houses to accommodate that number of wells and no more. That solved his problem. And he learned a fact Americans have not had to face in our history until now. He learned that there is nothing on earth to compare with growing population as a force for change. He learned that our rapidly growing population here at home has already changed our lives, so that freedom is not quite the same in a nation of one hundred and ninety million Americans as it was in an America of only four million people.

That incident in America was a small-scale version of what has been happening in other parts of the world, where rapidly growing populations have completely disrupted old ideas and old ways of doing things. This has gone far enough in Central and Southeast Asia, and in Latin America, to change even the symbol of our time. Until very recently, that symbol for most of the rest of the world was a man hungry for food. In most places it still is, but with a difference. What was it, what is it now, for you?

If you were asked to choose a symbol, a sign of the time in which you live, what would your choice be? The hydrogen bomb? A rocket, or space satellite? A scientist, or a machine of some kind? From our perch high up on our standard of living, in the most powerful nation on earth, would you recognize the symbol of our time in the men and women and children around the world who are now hungry for knowledge? If you did, it would be the symbol that represents best what is happening this minute to change the world you live in. The symbol of our time is a man, woman, or child, sitting in primitive classrooms, or in the open air, from the mountains of Bolivia to the jungles of Borneo, learning to read and write.

One of the most important facts in our present, affecting our future here in North America, is the statistic which shows that three of every five people on earth today cannot read or write. When World War II ended in 1945, the count was four of every five. The really remarkable thing about our time is that despite the addition of fifty million persons to the world's population every year since the end of World War II, the number of illiterate human beings has gone down. And it is about to go down even faster as such efforts as the Peace Corps stress teaching people to read and write. The Peace Corps has received more requests for teachers to do this job than for people to tackle any other problem. For any kind of advanced economic development, to make better lives possible for people in what we call the underdeveloped places, people must know how to read instructions and how to write reports.

The first step up the ladder to our kind of industrial civilization is the written word. And yet, strange as it may seem, we are not prepared for a world that is becoming more literate.

More and more people are hungry for answers to political and economic questions. So far we haven't really given them many answers, and for this reason, our teaching the illiterate people of the world to read and write could create a situation that could hurt us. We faced much the same problem in our public health programs which saved millions of lives, and yet

turned against us because we did not give those lives something to live for. The need is great to work out some way to
pass on our ideas, particularly our political and economic
ideas, as well as our alphabet. The new push we are giving
to the drive against illiteracy in the world—through agencies
like our Peace Corps—will open a new battleground on which
the battle for men's minds will inevitably be fought.

Most of those three out of five people who cannot read or
write still have a long way to go to reach the Twentieth Century. Until now people in such places have been affected
mainly by two things: medicines and pesticides to control
disease, and the knowledge that through science and technology they can live better lives.

Both can make the new battleground for men's minds very
dangerous for us, unless we are prepared to give people in
other places the political and economic information they will
need to make science and technology work for them; and if
they are not to be harmed, more than helped, by disease
control.

The fact is that many newly independent people *have* been
harmed more than helped by Twentieth Century ideas. Consider Egypt, for example.

Until 1947 the people of Egypt did not know much about
the benefits of tools, and machines, and disease control. They
know about those things, but they are not quite as happy
about them as we are. This does not mean they object to penicillin and sulfa drugs, or pesticides, to control disease; or that
they object to better farming tools that will grow more food
to fight hunger.

Egyptian parents are just as anxious as parents anywhere
are to have their children live through childhood. They do
not object to lowering the death rate; but they have good reason to object to the results of this that they have seen so far.

As we saw in Chapter Thirteen, the population of Egypt
has been growing, as ours has, but that growth has meant

lower living standards for them. The reason for this is not difficult to understand once the facts are straight. Egypt is a land with a total land area of about two hundred and fifty million acres. That makes it about equal in size to Texas plus New Mexico.

Egypt's population is more than twenty-seven million people, compared to some ten million persons spread out over Texas and New Mexico. So, at first glance, there appears to be more than twice as many people in Egypt living on what seems to be an equal amount of land.

Well, that first glance is dead wrong. Twenty-seven million Egyptians can't spread out over Egypt the way Americans do over Texas and New Mexico. All but some five and a half million acres of Egypt's land is useless, rainless desert that cannot be used productively.

Egypt's twenty-seven million people have to live and work, for the most part on five and a half million acres, practically all of it along the Nile River. Five and one-half million acres is about the size of our smallest state, Rhode Island. What do you suppose Rhode Island would be like if it had to support twenty-seven million people instead of eight hundred thousand?

Would it be possible to live the same kind of lives, enjoy the same kind of individual liberties and prosperity, or have the same kind of individual ideas about political matters under those conditions? Not likely. Freedom and democracy, as we have known them, have always had one very special ingredient—elbow room. Our kind of freedom and democracy need space. Heavily populated places like Egypt and Great Britain do not have that space. No reason is more important to explain why they don't have quite our kind of freedom either.

In a particularly important way for us Egypt is a type study, a sort of warning signal for us of what can happen any place where too many people live on too little good land. Egypt's problem of imbalance between numbers of people and the available resources is the same problem that the housing contractor had to work out in his Connecticut town. He did it by controlling the number of houses that could be built on a given amount of available land; and that word "available" should be stressed.

It should be stressed because even though science has a great capacity for solving problems (given plenty of time and huge amounts of money), there is only one way that twenty-seven million people can live on the amount of land available in Egypt today. And that is the way most Egyptians are living right now—in poverty.

Growing numbers of peoples around us are looking for political and economic answers to growing problems. We have not been giving them answers. The simple reason is, we haven't been able to decide what to say.

What political answers could we give to the world? Do we give the conservative answers of a Goldwater of Arizona, or the liberal answers of a Douglas of Illinois?

There would be no end of squabbling over that problem. Naturally it has been much easier to ignore it.

What economic things could we say to the world? Would we suggest the sort of planned economy an overpopulated Britain tried, or would we go down the line for private enterprise and our capitalist economy?

There would be no end to squabbling over that also. Naturally, it is much easier to avoid it.

And what can we say to the world about its population problems? Just think of the squabblings we could get into over that!

Then think of the fact that this nation was not built by men who feared squabbling or controversy. Its future will not be made secure from enemies by fearful men, either.

CHAPTER 19

Bombs, Babies, and Biology—III

MOST AMERICANS have always taken for granted the idea that among other peoples, particularly among Asians, there is less respect for human life than in the western nations. American troops in Korea, in 1950, were convinced of this after going through attacks by masses of Chinese troops who moved against their positions in waves, showing little or no concern about their losses. When the first wave of attackers was cut down, another would replace it. Time after time, Chinese gains were made over a carpet of their own dead. Many of our troops were sickened by the slaughter.

Americans in Asia had for many years been sickened. They were unable to understand this lack of respect for life. They learned that children were sold into slavery or prostitution by their parents. There was almost casual indifference to the sick and the poor who roamed the streets uncared for. Americans saw this in main cities and towns throughout Asia.

This is still true today in much of that part of the world. It has been particularly hard for Americans to understand.

In the late 1700s and the early 1800s when Americans began moving into what seemed to be an unused and empty continent, human life was highly valued and respected among the settlers. There were so few people around, and there was so much empty space.

People needed each other then to fight loneliness, their Indian enemies, and sickness. They needed each other to help settle and make useful all that empty space that was America.

When the great American migration westward began soon after the American Revolution, there were about four million people in this nation. On the frontier, and in the villages and towns, a high value was placed on the individual. He was important then. His descendants, in an American nation of about one hundred and ninety million people, are not as important today.

To understand that fact and why it is so, consider the case of John Q. Colonial, early American. In the year 1789, he lived in a small town not far from Boston, Mass., where the voting population was three hundred and fifteen persons. When, in 1789, the town government voted on the matter of building a new school, and a bridge to replace the ferry across the river nearby, John Q. Colonial had 1/315th part of the final decision whether or not those things would be done.

As a member of that small community, his influence as an individual over the final decision was considerably greater than the influence of his great-great-grandson John Q. American, in the affairs of the same town in the 1960s. In John Q. American's time, less than two hundred years later, the voting population had increased to thirty-one thousand five hundred persons. When, in the 1960s, the town government voted on the matter of building a new high school, and a highway by-passing the town to relieve its traffic problems, John Q.

American had only 1/31,500th part of the decision whether or not those things would be done.

In other words, in that space of years, the value of the individual as a voter in that community had dropped. John Q. American's vote had only one hundredth the influence his ancestor John Q. Colonial had. The personal significance of John Q. American as a free individual had declined.

The significance of freedom had also changed in those years. But John Q. American does not have to go back to the time of his great-great-grandfather to know that freedom isn't what it used to be.

John Q. Junior could remember the days in the early 1930s when the road that passed the family home had been a gravel-topped, two-lane affair. In those days, he had often jumped into the family car and backed it out on that road with hardly a glance to see whether or not it was clear of traffic.

In those days, a hundred cars passing either way on any day would have been considered unusually heavy traffic. Between his home and the city about twenty miles away there was one stoplight, and no stop signs on any of the access roads.

Today John Q. Junior would not dare back his car out on that road without taking great care to watch for traffic. That two-lane gravel road has become a four-lane paved highway sprinkled with stop lights and bordered by stop signs on every access road. Today, a hundred cars an hour is considered unusually light traffic. John Q. Junior knows that now he can't behave the way he used to on that road. His freedom has been curtailed by the large growth in traffic. He is much more restricted in what he can do simply because of the increase in number of cars.

This brings us back to our discussion in the last chapter: The force of growing numbers of people.

For most of the rest of the human race this means too many people trying to live on too little good land. In such places human values change; no matter what the religion, the kind of civilization, the culture, or the history of the people involved. In such places anywhere, people lose their value as individuals.

One such place is New York City, where one day a policeman chased a suspect down a side street. When the suspect failed to stop, the officer fired a warning shot. A twenty-five-year-old bystander happened to be in the way of that warning bullet. He was killed. That story was given one and a half inches in the back pages of a New York City newspaper during the summer of 1961.

In a city of many millions of people, blotting out one individual's life is not important any more. It hardly rates mention. In our country, too, not just in Asia, people are losing their value as individuals.

In Britain about fifty million people live on a land base of fifty-six million acres. The day is not far off when there will be one person for each acre of land in that nation.

In case those figures sound like meaningless numbers, the same proportion of Americans to our total number of acres would mean an American population of more than two billion people, instead of our current one hundred and ninety million.

We are, by contrast with England, still an underpopulated country. In a heavily populated England, the London City Council talks about ways of "disposing of its overspill." That means what to do with the growing number of Britons that London can't hold.

Today, that "overspill" is people, but there are so many of them in and around London that they aren't referred to as people anymore. They become a bit of scientific jargon. They become "overspill."

In such places, a long way from Asia, people lose their value as individuals. One of the main reasons for this, everywhere, is the loss of living space. The price paid by the British has overtones that would be very similar to many Asian peoples.

With increasing numbers of people living cheek to jowl in the western nations, it seems the public welfare becomes more important than individual rights. Property owners in many cities around the United States found out, quite recently, that their private property rights went out when the state stepped in with its right of eminent domain, to relocate highways, and redevelop slum and blighted areas.

Whether those changes are good or bad is not the point here. The point is that increasing the numbers of people anywhere, East or West, changes the value of people, even to the point where parents in certain heavily overpopulated places in Asia will sell their children into slavery or worse, because they can't support them. The money they get helps keep the remaining children alive.

This does not mean those Asian parents love their children any less. It means those overpopulated places know poverty Americans can't even imagine. Poverty-stricken people simply do not have the means to care for their sick and poor, the same sick and poor that Americans have seen, and can still see, uncared for, on the streets of cities and towns all over Asia. There is a lack of respect for life wherever life is degraded by too many people.

No group of men were more dedicated to the idea of dignified lives than those of John Q. Colonial's day in revolutionary America. They were convinced such dignity was possible in this country, for various reasons. Possibly the strongest reason was the one expressed by Tom Paine in his pamphlet, *Common Sense,* where he wrote: "Our present numbers are so happily proportioned to our wants that no man need be idle."

What he wrote about was an unusual and happy circumstance. There were few nations or peoples, even in Tom Paine's time, so well favored that the numbers of people did not exceed the ability of the economy to meet their needs.

That happy circumstance had a great deal to do with the rise of Europe and North America as the centers for world power, particularly after industry became the basis of power in the world. That was also the point in time, during the Seventeenth Century, when population began to increase in Europe, as new farming tools and agricultural ideas turned out more food to support more people.

At that time, the North American colonies were one of the main dumping grounds for the "overspill" of Europe. Enough people left the Old World for North America, Australia, and South Africa to maintain a low rate of population growth in the home countries. That meant a happy balance between people and their needs and wants, in Europe as well as in America.

In America, we were never to be bothered by the problem of too many people, or a population growing faster than our industrial economy grew. Throughout practically our whole development into an industrial nation we never had enough people. The story of Europe's and America's industrial development is one of fast-growing economies staying ahead of population growth. Europe's ability to get rid of its excess population, by sending it all over the world, was a critical part of that success story.

People in Asia have been trying to work out a solution to the same problem since the end of World War II. But there was not in the past, and there is not now, a happy balance for them between the numbers of people and their needs.

Unlike the western countries, the nations in Asia are not starting to industrialize with small populations. Practically all of them are heavily populated, or overpopulated, as they start. There are no empty Americas or Canadas, or Australias left to take their overspill, to give their economies the time to get ahead of population growth. Most other places in the world are, in fact, closed to them.

Some still underpopulated places like Canada and the United States have quota systems, letting in only so many Asians every year. Other places have exclusion acts, keeping them out entirely.

A country like communist China would have to export between eight and ten million people a year, in order to keep the mainland's population growth low enough to give its economy a chance to get ahead, as ours once did. It would take most of the ships and planes now in existence, working around the clock every day of the year, just to move that number of human beings assuming there was any place on earth that could take that number of people for any length of time. There is no such place.

For this reason alone, an explosive situation is building up in practically all the non-industrial nations of Asia. It could easily explode into revolution, resulting in a very different kind of world from what we would like to see. Economic development for such nations can't be modeled after our own experience. The conditions are entirely different, and they call for entirely different methods from those we, in America, have thought about, or are thinking about even now.

This point was made quite clear by President Ayub Khan of Pakistan, when he came to the United States in 1961.

Ayub Khan took over the government of Pakistan in 1958. At that time, that country had received about a billion dollars from us, in what was called foreign aid. We were putting out enough money every year to cover about forty per cent of Pakistan's entire budget. But in 1958, despite our money and aid, Pakistan was turning out less food per person than it had produced when the nation was created in 1947.

It had just imported one and a half million tons of grain, to hold off starvation. Its factories were working part time or not at all, because of shortages of raw materials. The country's income was about fifty dollars per person per year, at a time when ours was over two thousand dollars per person per year.

Since Ayub Khan took power in Pakistan, he has forced reforms, planned new ways to tackle economic development, and his people have worked hard just to stand still economi-

cally. Pakistanis ate up or used up whatever additional wealth
that country's economy could produce.

Population growth was defeating the President's efforts to
bring about economic development in his country, and population growth is one more important reason why ninety billions
of dollars in American foreign aid spent all over the world
has not accomplished the goals we sought.

America could no longer afford to be neutral about the
problem of population growth, Ayub Khan told President Kennedy. At this stage, America's security was at stake too. We
had to act to help Pakistan, and other nations, to solve their
population problems.

Were we prepared to do this, the Pakistani President asked?
And are we?

No nation has done more than the United States, for so long
a time, to make the industrial idea clear to the world's non-
industrial peoples. Our technicians, engineers, and other
trained persons have set up industrial operations and intro-
duced new agricultural ways of doing things based on machines and factories. They have raised hopes for better lives
everywhere. Yet those hopes are not being realized by growing numbers of people.

In frustration and disappointment those we have helped
have become dangerous to us. And then, to complicate matters further, there's our stress on reading and writing. Karl
Marx once wrote quite a bit about just how dangerous people
could be who were disappointed by the industrial process.
They could become the cadre of communist revolutionaries.

The fact is that we have not done enough of the necessary
things that can be done to make economic development a
reality for those we are trying to help.

The fact is that growing numbers of frustrated people,
newly literate, have been reading communist writings and ac-
cepting more and more technical aid from communist countries.

The fact is that the communist world has been helped by the growing frustrations of growing numbers of people all over the world.

The fact is that, as Ayub Khan of Pakistan pointed out, the population problem alone can be the key to victory for communism.

Most of the arguments and the discussions about the population explosion today turn on the largely irrelevant question of how many people could live on this planet. Five billion? Twenty-five billion? A hundred and ten billion?

This has always been an interesting, safe dispute amongst us as long as it did not touch political, social, economic, philosophical or religious matters.

But it is an argument that does have an answer. That answer is not based on the statistical calculations of mathematicians, economists, sociologists or demographers. It is based on three simple facts: sunlight, chlorophyll in plants, and land. Land on which sunlight and chlorophyll in plants can react to produce the organic carbon that is life for man on this planet.

Not all land will grow plants to produce organic carbon. Some land is too cold—up in the Arctic. Some land is too high —in mountain country. Some is too dry. And much of the land that supports plant life will not support food plants.

But assume that some day science will find a way to convert every plant on this planet into a source of organic carbon and thus into food for men. What then? Plants can convert only so much sunlight, and human beings eating those plants can get only so much food value from them. Using all the earth's greenery this way, the earth could probably support at least thirty times as many people as it does today.

But the most important thing is, not how many people the earth can support, but what kind of lives would they have to live?

CHAPTER 20

The Explosive Word

WHEN AMERICAN and Soviet tanks were brought into position with guns trained across the wall dividing Berlin in August, 1961, the question that raced around the world was— War of nerves or the real thing? American and Soviet power have been displayed in that explosive place many times since the end of World War II, because each side claims that the other has violated either the terms or the spirit of the agreement that put them in Berlin. That agreement resulted from a conference held in Potsdam in 1945, when the "Big Four" Allies met to do something that could not be done.

If the nations represented at that conference had come with no special axes to grind, with the purest motives and the best intentions, it would still have been extremely difficult to reach a workable agreement about ways to deal effectively with a defeated Germany, or anything else. There was a built-in obstacle at that conference. It was the same obstacle that has been built into every conference in which the western powers have tried to reach agreements with the U.S.S.R. Few Americans recognized it, or were prepared to deal with it, despite the fact that we have faced that particular obstacle many times in our history.

One such occasion was the signing of a treaty in the late 1800s between the United States and the Apache Indians. The place was not far from Tombstone, Arizona, and it was a very important treaty. It stipulated that there would be no more fighting in that part of the West between those Indians and the settlers moving westward. The Apaches had been defeated at last after some of the hardest fighting of the Indian wars, and the victorious commander of the federal forces in that territory had arranged the treaty-signing conference to climax that event.

As treaty-signings go, there was nothing particularly strange about that conference, for the United States troops. They had experienced it before, several times. It was the usual way to end wars. Their commanding officer, as a representative of the United States, worked out the terms of the treaty, and he was prepared to sign it. All that was needed to complete this perfectly normal routine was that the Apache leader should agree to the terms of that treaty by signing it as the representative of the Apache people. All this was in accord with tradition and correct procedure; tradition and procedure that made sense at least to the colonel and his troops.

Unfortunately, it made little sense to the Apaches.

The Apache leader did sign the treaty. He signed several copies, in fact. He got one copy, the colonel got one, and the ceremony was over.

Off went the Apaches. The troops headed off in the other direction—and weren't heard from again, because the next morning, as they slept late after celebrating the end of their troubles with the Apaches, an Apache war party came into their camp and slaughtered every one of them. When their bodies were found a few days later by a scouting party, the colonel's copy of the treaty, which said that the Apaches would not fight any more, was still in his dispatch case.

This is an incident in American history. What did it prove? Well, as far as Americans of that day were concerned, it proved that the Apache could not be trusted. It proved that Apaches did not live up to their agreements. They did not honor their word.

Americans were wrong. There was a built-in obstacle to that treaty-signing incident between the Apaches and those troops which made it impossible for those Indians to live up to their part of that agreement. The obstacle was in a word, and an idea.

The word was "leader," and the mistaken idea was that an Apache leader could represent all of his people, as that army colonel could represent all the American people. There was no such national leader of the Apaches at that point in history.

There were groups of Apaches, and each had its own leader; much as we have fifty states each with its own leader.

Suppose an invading enemy forced the governor of California to sign a treaty which said that thereafter all fighting between America and that enemy would stop. Would it?

The governor of California could not speak for all Americans, as that Apache leader of one war party could not speak for other Apache war parties, one of which wiped out those troops.

Yesterday's Americans did not know that fact; did not consider it important enough to know about. The price of that ignorance was paid in lives. That incident proved, not that Apaches couldn't be trusted, but that it is dangerous to take for granted the idea that words mean the same thing to all people.

But words mean different things to different people, no matter how carefully they are juggled in Indian treaties or

Potsdam conferences. This fact has cropped up time after time in human affairs right from the start.

For example, Og the Caveman and his tribe five hundred thousand years ago faced a very serious problem. It was more than he and his people could tackle and work out themselves. They needed help, so they went to their neighbors, Ab and his tribe, to discuss their dangerous problem. As it happened, Ab was very much interested in Og's story because he had been thinking about it himself. Ab's tribe also faced the problem of danger, and it was more than they could tackle alone.

The two tribes discussed the matter and reached an agreement. We agree, they said, to work together to solve our problem of danger. They both used the same word in their agreement—danger. They shook hands to seal the deal, and went off to their respective territories.

A very short time later, Ab accused Og of failure to live up to the terms of the agreement, while Og wasted no words in charging that it was Ab who was responsible for what went wrong.

What did go wrong? They were using the same words to mean very different things.

Og's tribe lived in a river valley, in caves along the banks of a river. Every year, the river would flood. It would threaten the lives of his tribe. Og wanted to tackle that danger by building dikes, walls along the river to keep it from overflowing. His tribe could not do that job alone. They had gone to Ab for the help they needed.

But Ab's tribes lived in caves on the side of a mountain, and every year avalanches came crashing down the side of that mountain, threatening the lives of his people. Ab wanted to tackle that danger by building breastworks, walls over their caves to keep the mountain from sealing them off and possibly killing them. Ab's tribe could not do that job alone, and they had been happy at the prospect of getting Og's help to tackle that danger.

But when both sides began to carry out the terms of their agreement, they had very different ideas about how to do it. Danger meant drowning to Og. Danger meant being crushed by avalanche to Ab. It was the same word, but it had very different meanings.

Do not get the idea that this very simple example has no meaning in our lives. Take a Russian dictionary and an English dictionary. You can translate words from one of these books into the other in writing agreements or treaties with the U.S.S.R., but you cannot always transfer meanings with those words. Behind each word is a different kind of history, different experiences, different ways of doing things.

For this reason, as stated earlier, if the western nations and the U.S.S.R. were to sit down at a conference table without a single ulterior motive, both sides would still have considerable trouble expressing what they meant by the words they used. When you add to this problem the fact that the U.S.S.R. has some clearly stated and often repeated ulterior motives in its dealings with us and the rest of the world—as we do, too, in a different way, dealing with them—it becomes difficult to reach agreements about anything. The record of the meetings between the Soviet Union and the western nations, over the past few years, makes that quite clear.

This does not mean that agreements cannot be reached with the U.S.S.R. or anyone else. It simply means that a built-in block has helped to make agreements with a Soviet Union hard, when not impossible.

Unfortunately, it is a problem most Americans, right up to our highest officials in Washington, have hardly thought about.

Until now we have had to deal with a world that was run for the most part by Englishmen, Frenchmen, Dutch, Portuguese, Belgians and other Europeans. They are peoples who have shared history, have had common experiences, and have done things in ways that have produced words and meanings that are very much the same from one language to another, from one people to another.

Take an American, a French, English, Dutch, or any other West European dictionary, and you will find that you can translate words from one of those languages to the others, with roughly the same meanings.

We had a fairly easy time signing treaties and agreements with people pretty much like ourselves, who spoke for Indians in India, for Bantus in Africa, for Malayans in Southeast Asia. But that easy time ended with World War II. Russia is not a newcomer to the affairs of Europe, but that country has never been a part of the history or the experience that make it possible for the nations of Europe to call themselves the "Western World."

The Soviet Union, since becoming a world power, has posed entirely new and different problems for us to face. They are challenging our leadership in a world of three thousand different language groups, spoken by people who now run their own affairs. People who are not at all like us, or like our friends in Europe.

Their language cannot be translated easily, the meaning of many of their words comes from ideas and concepts, in religion and politics, and economics, and social systems we have never known.

How we tackle and work out this problem will decide the shape of our future.

This is not a new problem in human affairs. It was faced and solved in a way particularly important to Americans today by a man named Arminius who, in the year 9 A.D., tampered mightily with history. He was chief of the Cherusci, a Slavic people, and his home was near the Rhine River in what is presently Germany, in a place called the Teutoburger Forest. One day he kept certain evil men from carrying some alien ideas into his home territory.

Most of his neighbors in the Europe of those days feared

those men because, among other things, they wanted to dominate the world. By 9 A.D., Romans did, in fact, dominate a sizeable part of it. They were about to push north and take over the British Isles. They had already pushed across most of what is called Western Europe today. They held most of the territory around the Mediterranean Sea. And in 9 A.D., they headed into the Teutoburger Forest, pushing east to take over lands that might have included some people living around the Pripet Marshes in Eastern Europe.

Arminius kept them from reaching those people. He was not one to froth at the mouth uselessly about the evils of Romanism. He knew the Roman system worked. He knew the Roman Empire was getting stronger every day. He had studied Romanism, had been educated in Rome, and he knew how it worked and why.

And on that day in 9 A.D., he used that knowledge to defeat' Roman troops in the Teutoburger Forest in one of history's most significant battles.

The Roman Empire stopped moving east at that point on the map. They never reached the Pripet Marshes. As a result, the Slavs, who in a few years were to push out of those marshes to the east and take over Russia, did not learn about the Twelve Tablets of the Roman law, or the *comitia* or the *tributa,* and the *comitia centuriata.* Only the Europeans who were dominated by the Roman Empire west of the Rhine River were to know about them.

For those people in Western Europe, the Twelve Tablets of the law, written in Rome in 451 B.C., became the basis for systems of law and justice that outlived the Roman Empire, and have extended into our time. Our ideas today about law and justice in the United States have roots that go back to those tablets. Many of the ideas about government that Alexander Hamilton, James Madison, and John Jay, expressed in our *Federalist Papers,* go back to those *comitias,* and the assemblies and senates of Rome.

Those ideas were not forced on the Slavic peoples to become a part of their lives, as they had been forced upon the nations of the western world who were once dominated by the Roman tyranny. Instead, Russians carry the stamp of a different tyranny, one that came roaring out of the east, from Mongolia, during the 1200s. The Russians of that day saw those men as evil too, intent on dominating the world. The Mongols dominated more of it at the peak of their power than did the Romans, and their hold on the Russian part of it was to last about two hundred and fifty years. During that time, the Russians were forced by a Mongol tyranny to accept ideas about law and justice, and government, that were just as complicated and highly developed as those of Rome, but different.

From the Great Khan, who was an absolute autocrat heading a despotic, centralized—or totalitarian—government, the Russians inherited their "Great Prince" idea and kept it even after they broke the hold of the Mongol Empire. The mark of that experience is very much a part of communist Russia's ideas today, about the proper legal, political, social, and economic way to deal with the world. This covers everything from Potsdam conferences to disarmament conferences, and from Berlin to Laos. At such conferences, words become dangerously explosive things in treaties or agreements of any kind. Words do not mean the same things to the two groups of people.

Proof that they do not mean the same thing is starkly clear in a number of special books published in the U.S.S.R. Every word contained in them has been approved by a committee of the Communist Party. The job of that committee is to see to it that words are used as powerful weapons to do as the Romans and Mongols did in their day: to dominate the world.

One of those special books can be purchased in most bookstores in the U.S.S.R. today. It is called *A Dictionary of Political Terms*. To see how different the meanings of words can be, read some of its definitions for words like freedom, de-

mocracy, republic, individualism, conservative, and liberal.
You will not recognize or accept the definitions; but the important thing is that for all communists, everywhere, until
very recently, these definitions were the only definitions to be
used in conferences, propaganda, and education.

Very recently, the communist Chinese have begun changing
the meaning for some words like freedom and democracy.
They have a different stamp of history and experience to influence their ideas about political, social, and economic matters. While this does not change the goals of either communist
state, it does change their approach to those goals.

The communists use this approved definition method for
making very clear what they mean by the words they use. In
this way, they pass on legal, political, social and economic
ideas to the newly independent people using more than three
thousand different languages all over the world. When those
people turn to us for such ideas to help set up independent
governments for themselves, they often get conflicting answers from Americans who are not agreed about the meaning
of their own words.

What, for example, do you mean by the words *conservative*,
or *liberal*, or *communist*, or *democracy?* Is your definition the
same as your neighbors?

How would you define two words for an Asian or an African, two words that represent a new way of life for him, the
words *democratic republic?* These two key words are explained for him in great detail in the Soviet dictionary.

The communists have been setting up what they call "democratic republics" wherever they gain control, because the
words have an enormously powerful appeal to practically the
whole world. Such countries are, of course, neither democratic
nor republics.

But what can you say about these two words when there
are Americans amongst us who have decided that somehow
certain Americans don't belong with certain other Americans?

One of the more interesting and irrelevant squabbles of the 1960s in the United States is whether this country is a republic or a democracy. It is interesting because it points up just how dangerous it can be not to know the meaning of our own words. In this world words are dynamite.

When the Founding Fathers set up a republic in America toward the end of the Eighteenth Century, they described it as "the delegation of government to a small number of citizens, elected by the rest." In their day this did not mean "rule of the people" which is the root meaning of the word democracy. In their day a universal suffrage did not exist.

Since then things have changed. Women now have the right to vote. Negroes, Chinese, Mexicans, Japanese, and a host of others among us have achieved that right. And by this extension of the right to vote we have evolved into a constitutional, representative democracy. The people rule in America through a universal suffrage, "by delegating government to a small number of citizens elected by the rest": the very words used by the Founding Fathers to describe our form of government in our Federalist Papers. We are a republic, and we most certainly are a democracy.

An army colonel in the late 1880s did not know the word *leader* meant something different to an Apache Indian from what it meant to him. He and his men died as the price of that ignorance. Arminius the Cherusci knew what the Romans meant in his time. He defeated that tyranny with his knowledge.

The Soviet *Dictionary of Political Terms* mentioned earlier is part of a series that deals with economic, social, military, trade, scientific, philosophical, and other terms as well. In those books are the words being used now all over the world by our communist competitors for world leadership. They are used effectively in cultural exchange programs, propaganda, and international conferences to shape the world into a communist kind of place.

It is that kind of knowledge that today's American must have if we are to do with our knowledge what Arminius the Cherusci did with his knowledge to defeat Rome. Whether today's Arminius is an American corporation president, or a college student touring the world, he cannot fight this battle until he knows how to explain himself to the world. More important than that is the need to explain ourselves to ourselves.

One of the most important battlegrounds right now is the American classroom. Tomorrow's Americans must know that words are explosive things. They must know that language is a weapon in today's world. They must know what we mean by the words we use. When any nation reaches that point in its affairs at which it cannot explain itself to its own children, it has no future.

CHAPTER 21

Words and Survival

LING CHEN, Chinese fisherman, made headlines around the world one night early in 1955.

Ling was lost. While trying to find his way home, he paddled his sampan into a restricted defense area just off the Chinese nationalist island of Matsu. The sentries on Matsu saw him, and they fired a few warning shots over his head to get him out of there. He got out fast—and left a problem in his wake.

A U.S. Army observer on Matsu saw that incident involving a single Chinese sampan, and the next morning you read about a "fleet" of Chinese communist "war junks," carrying many men, sailing to Matsu in an invasion attempt. Those few warning shots were reported as a night-long battle during which the invasion was turned back, after many communist ships and men were destroyed.

What you read and heard in the news that morning was not

true. What you read and heard that morning was "managed news." Deadly stuff.

Late in the fall of 1957, the President of the United States spoke to the nation in a special telecast to explain where we stood in the race for space with the Soviet Union. A month earlier, the U.S.S.R. had placed Sputnik I into orbit around the earth, taking man's first step into space. The American nation had not been prepared for this Soviet accomplishment. We were troubled. If we were behind Russia, how far behind were we? What were we doing to catch up?

President Eisenhower briefed the nation about what had been done, what was being done and what would be done. It was a reassuring talk. At no point was it more reassuring than when the President pointed to a kind of pyramid-shaped object several feet tall near his desk, and announced that it was a nose cone. It had been recovered from a long-range missile which had come back to the earth's surface after traveling hundreds of miles into outer space.

"Here it is," President Eisenhower said, "completely undamaged. Intact. Our scientists and engineers have solved that problem."

That announcement made headlines. It meant that America had made as important a step toward man's eventual exploration of space as Russia had in sending Sputnik I into orbit.

That announcement meant we were not far behind the Russians. We were simply working on another part of a big problem. There, in the nose cone next to the President was proof. We had solved the re-entry problem. The U.S.S.R. may have been first to put a satellite in space but we were the first to bring an object back from space. Now we knew that one day a man could be brought back from space.

All this was quite clear in President Eisenhower's special telecast that night in November, 1957. Few of the nation's newspapers failed to carry that story; the part about the nose cone, at least. The President's facts had been given to him by the Defense Department. It was a good thing to hear. It made everybody feel much better about where we stood in the space race against Communist Russia.

There was only one thing wrong with that announcement. It was not true.

It was "managed news." Deadly stuff, particularly dangerous to a free people concerned about staying free.

Mr. Eisenhower did not himself manage the news about the nose cone in that special telecast. He was as much the victim of managed news as you or I. The unstated but essential fact about that nose cone was that it had come back from outer space into the earth's atmosphere at a speed slower than was required for an operational long-range missile.

At that lower speed, the re-entry problem had not been solved. It has been solved since then. It was not solved at the time of that telecast. You were not given the facts.

This touches the heart of the problem President Kennedy pointed up in several speeches in 1961. The gist of his remarks was: "The more I get to know the facts, the more I am convinced that we face the hour of maximum danger in our history, the problem of the survival of our way of life; not so much because of what the communists are doing to win the future, but because of what we are not willing to do."

This was strong talk, and it led to a strong question. According to testimony given before the House Subcommittee on Government Information, there are now more than a million Americans in government who have the right to mark documents "secret"; to keep you from knowing the facts of what President Kennedy has called America's "hour of maximum danger."

What you miss are not facts about how to build a hydrogen bomb, or missile guidance systems, or where our ICBM sites are located. These are operational facts which no sensible American would want to know about, or would expect to know about, for obvious security reasons.

The "secret" stamp is used widely in government now to keep you from knowing about things that have nothing to do with security, ranging from statistics about peanut production to information about the states over which migratory birds fly every year. Information is kept "secret" about the kind of furniture we put into our military transport planes, as well as the names of farmers paid not to grow certain foods under agricultural programs.

"Managed news" cannot pass on to the average American citizen the sense of urgency, the sense of danger to our way of life that leaders in our government from President Kennedy on down know. How can Americans be concerned about the real problems the nation faces, if they are given only such facts as certain people or agencies in and out of government decide they should know? Is it possible that what a free people in a free society do not know can hurt them?

Secrecy has been an important question in this nation almost from the start. Thomas Jefferson was concerned with it when he asked Philip Freneau to come to Philadelphia in 1791.

Philip Freneau played an enormously important, but little-known part in American history, the part of critic, through his newspaper, the *National Gazette*.

Jefferson asked Freneau to set up shop in Philadelphia, which was the nation's capital at the time, because the young republic wasn't going so well. There were strong pressures in the United States to have the republic changed into a monarchy. Those pressures were particularly strong in Philadelphia, where they were backed by a Federalist newspaper.

Freneau became this nation's first opposition editor. He proved Jefferson's faith that in a free market of ideas, in the competition of ideas, lay the safeguards of the republic. Freneau's criticism, according to Jefferson, saved the republic. Freneau showed the power a critical press could have in public affairs.

Now, the important thing to note about that historical episode is that word "criticism." That word played an important part in saving this democratic republic at another, earlier hour of maximum danger in our affairs.

Right at the heart of today's hour of maximum danger is the fact that the word "criticize" has become a dirty word. To criticize, for those who do not know, is to condemn. But any good dictionary will point out that the word has two meanings, the more important of which is to *evaluate with knowledge*. It means to review, with knowledge; to question, with knowledge; to get at the facts; to get at the truth. All through American history the Philip Freneaus of our free press have criticized in our hours of maximum danger; through wars, national scandals, corruption from the Boss Tweeds to the Hoffas. It has been an important word in the history of this nation. It is one of the more neglected, misused words in the nation today.

Criticism was neglected and unused in that nose cone incident back in 1957, as it is in the growing problem of "managed news" right now.

It is neglected by a very special group of Americans who have a license to exercise a special responsibility. The license was granted to that special group—the press—by the First Amendment; the responsibility rests with the press to safeguard the republic.

But how many members of the press knew enough about the new science of rockets and missiles to spot the Defense Department's "managed news" about the re-entry problem back in 1957?

How many news men are prepared now to "evaluate with knowledge" the kind of news that is given out about our space program, or about our place in the world as a science power? How many journalists, editors, and publishers understand and really believe what Thomas Jefferson said when he welcomed Philip Freneau to Philadelphia as an opposition editor back in 1791, "that a popular government, without popular information or the means to get it, is but a prologue to a farce, a tragedy, or both"?

How many journalists, editors and publishers know, particularly those in the twenty states of this country where, as this is being written, not a single city has an opposition newspaper, that Thomas Jefferson's words were never truer than they are in our time?

In 1931, a very few Americans, perhaps numbering dozens, knew that just outside the Manchurian village of Wan-Pao-Shan the prologue to a tragedy was written on the morning of June 27. It began when Captain Nakamura of the Imperial Japanese Army was shot and killed by a Chinese soldier.

That shot was not important enough to be mentioned in the American press in 1931. But by 1941 the story was very much in our news. Ten years later, partly because of what had happened to a man Americans did not know, in a place they had never heard of, their lives were disrupted, and their world changed permanently.

That bullet fired in 1931 touched off the Chinese-Japanese war, which led directly to Pearl Harbor. There was a direct line from a Japanese Army officer killed in 1931 to three hundred and ninety thousand Americans killed during World War II. This was not clear to us before Pearl Harbor, but there was every reason to think it would be self-evident after World War II.

Then something happened, again in China, which made it very clear that the lessons of Captain Nakamura and World War II had not been learned. European history books describe what happened as the second "ten days that shook the world."

In the city of Chungking two men met to decide what may some day be seen as the most fateful conference in world history. The two men were Chou En-lai, who became the premier of communist China, and Chiang Kai-shek.

The reporters covering that conference found it heavy going, dialectical, hard to understand; harder to make understandable for readers in America.

It was much harder to explain than the Chinese egg trick, which several foreign correspondents saw a Chinese magician perform on a side street one day while taking a break from the conference.

The conference was breaking up. From its ashes came civil war and a communist China. You can read about what went on between Chou En-lai and Chiang Kai-shek in the few paragraphs that appeared in news reports that day across this country, but there were columns giving every detail of the Chinese technique of standing eggs on end.

That story about an egg trick almost pushed the story of the meeting out of the news at that critical point in world history.

Why?

Because as editors and publishers across this nation have been measuring your taste, and judging your interests in news, they believe you prefer it this way; to be amused and entertained by egg tricks rather than informed about a line of history extending from Chungking in faraway China to a possible World War III.

The egg trick, by the way, is quite a trick. Try it some time. Try balancing an egg on its end. It's quite a trick; but is this the kind of news you prefer? After the lesson of Pearl Harbor, and China, and Indo-China, and Cuba, and now Laos?

It is only a short step from the people in the press who hold that view of your tastes and intelligence, to the spreading of secrecy by people in government who do not believe you deserve the facts.

People in government in many cases are more afraid of that unthinking, amusement-bent public than of an enemy country. That is one of the reasons why what President Eisenhower called "Operation Candor" fell apart, in 1953, soon after he moved into the White House.

Mr. Eisenhower came into office with the same strong desire to put a stop to unnecessary secrecy in government as Mr. Kennedy did when he took office later.

In 1953, President Eisenhower put his White House staff to work for two months preparing a detailed report of the facts of political and economic life at home and abroad. But that report was never made public. A strong argument against it was that the kind of public interested in egg tricks, and the latest happenings in bars and brothels, would find the truth too unfamiliar, the facts too alarming. It was best not to stir up such people. Things were best left as they were.

Instead of "Operation Candor," letting the people know as much as possible about what was going on, there are numerous reports published by the House of Representatives Subcommittee on Government Information which shows government agencies cutting off more and more facts from the people. That alone explains why so few life-and-death facts are discussed or reported intelligently in the press. That alone can do much to explain why there is no informed, realistic public opinion to match President Kennedy's concern about the nation in its hour of maximum danger.

Nothing does more to make this the hour of maximum danger for the nation than the fact that the public is not informed about the nation's life-and-death problems. An informed, realistic public opinion was always intended to be the guardian of this democratic republic. The First Amendment was written into the Constitution to insure that there would always be a free press to keep the public informed.

At this point, it would be very easy to get involved in another egg question. The chicken or the egg: which comes first? Does the press decide what the public shall know, or does the public decide what the press shall print?

Well, where do we go from that point?

First, we go back to the Wan-Pao-Shans of the world, the Chungkings, Vientianes, the Havanas. They lead directly into our future. Outside of a few major cities, and the radio and television networks, most of the press simply isn't prepared to report that line of history, as it must be reported if we are to survive our hour of maximum danger.

There may be as many as twenty out of the eighteen hundred daily newspapers in the nation at this minute that have qualified foreign news editors. Qualified means men able to explain how and why the facts of life have changed for us. There are certainly no more than twenty.

In 1931, we were a self-contained nation with a national economy. We did not need the world around us.

Today, we are no longer a self-contained nation. We are at the center of the Free World with an international economy. We depend heavily on the world around us.

What the press cannot do to make this understandable and clear, our local and national clubs and organizations can do, from the Leagues of Women Voters to the Rotarians.

More than a few such organizations have formed study groups to do just this.

I worked with one such group for several months. They tackled an incident that occurred on the Pakistan-Indian border a few years ago.

A news report at that time simply told about an Indian plane shot down by Pakistani fighters. But buried in that incident was an enormously important story that touches directly on some of our most important problems, particularly in Asia.

We have no greater concern in Asia than preventing the spread of Chinese communist power. To this end, we have carried out a military assistance program to places like Pakistan for years.

It was some of that military power which we put into Pakistani hands that shot down that Indian plane. Our anti-communist policies against China were thereby weakened.

Chinese communist power is not just military. It is also economic, cultural, and political.

One of the most important battles for power in Asia since the end of World War II has been the competition between a communist China and India to see which nation could do the quickest and best job of catching up with the Twentieth Century. In China, economic development is enforced by the full power of the state. The needs of the people are kept down to a minimum. Whatever profits the Chinese economy produces are plowed back into new factories, new railroads, and new farms.

In India, economic development is planned, but not forced. All Asia, Africa, and South America have been watching that competition with great interest. Our own future will be affected very much by results of that competition. Over the years, during which there have been poor relations between Pakistan and India, we helped the Pakistanis balance their power against India. To offset that military power, most of which we supplied, India had to set aside money for weapons, money badly needed for economic development. Our policy to contain China's physical power by arming the Pakistanis as possible anti-communist allies worked against India's economic power.

This is the kind of analytical, interpretive stuff a free people must have if the power to make final decisions in public affairs is to stay in their hands. Americans are not getting it today.

A popular idea examined in many of our university classrooms is the "theory of least effort." All of human history, this theory holds, is one long drive by man to find ways to do more work with less effort. From the lever and the wheel in prehistoric time, to automatic computers today, the theory has worked in all ways but one. It has not worked where the human brain is concerned. To make today's enormously complicated technical society work demands more mental effort than ever before, not less.

That's what makes the topic we have considered in the final chapter so critical in our affairs today. Americans running the most complicated technical society in history are not being given information they need to keep it running.

If we fail, it will not make much difference over the long haul of history whether the government denied us the facts of life and death; or the press failed to inform us for whatever reason; or whether we simply did not want to be informed. Whatever the reason, the result can be the end of America's unique story.

What the founders of this nation contributed to that story in a colonial America, through an American revolution, has greater meaning today than it did then. The idea of popular government based on popular knowledge has greater meaning because the main issue of our time can be described as the power of example set by two kinds of civilization representing different stages of historical development in history. Thus, while the American Revolution was important at the time principally to Americans, it is of crucial importance now as the foundation of the example of government that we set for the entire world.

There are no written records to tell us when some men rebelled for the first time against the natural order of tyranny. Whatever their original reason may have been, their example has been followed by others right into our own period, by men who saw oppression and tyranny as great evils. Such men have made history a long and bloody story of the decentralization of power. Power to rule spread outward and downward from Pharaohs, emperors, and despots, to the entire voting population which has and must use the power of government in the Twentieth Century kind of democracy that we know in these United States. That movement took the power to rule out of the hands of one person and placed it in various ways and at different times in the hands of small groups of men, oligarchies, until the action of colonial Americans led to a ruling power in the hands of the people.

That simple sequence is important because one issue of our

time is the power of example. Temporarily at least, America is the leading example of the kind of civilization in which the power to rule is the right of every voting citizen. The Soviet Union is currently the leading example of the kind of civilization in which the real ruling power is held by a small ruling group, a modern oligarchy representing a step backward to a more primitive political system. To a world full of newly independent states looking for answers to political, social, and economic problems, the American and Russian ways of life are being critically examined as possible answers to their problems.

The American answer is not the easy one in the world today. It was never easy to carry out the risky idea that the power to govern was safest in the hands of the greatest number of free and responsible individuals. Those good men in an earlier America who fought and worked for that idea saw in it an end to the evil of oppression and tyranny. They were right. Good men in America now must fight and work every bit as hard, to make our experience with freedom meaningful to a world in revolt against similar evils.

About this, Edmund Burke spoke meaningfully to us in 1775, when he said: "All that is necessary for the forces of evil to win in the world is that enough good men do nothing."

ABOUT THE AUTHOR

Albert E. Burke, a native of New York, received his B.A. and M.A. from the University of California, and his Ph.D. in International Relations (International Aspects of Resource Use) from the University of Pennsylvania. He was the Director of Graduate Studies in Conservation and Resource Use at Yale University from 1951 to 1957. He lived and studied abroad for several years, spending varying periods of time in the U.S.S.R., Europe, and Asia. Dr. Burke and his wife have spent considerable time working and living with American Indians in Arizona, New Mexico, and California.

In 1957 he was appointed Educational Television Consultant for the National Broadcasting Company, where he produced the award-winning series *Survival*. *Probe,* the new television series begun in the fall of 1962, succeeds *A Way of Thinking*, Dr. Burke's earlier series, which aroused considerable interest throughout the United States.

It has been said that Dr. Burke's "out-of-school" education, through personal experience, has been more important in his life than his degrees or the positions he has held. He lives in Cheshire, Connecticut, with his wife, who teaches at the Yale Medical School, and his two children. His study is a converted trailer.

THIS BOOK WAS SET IN

CALEDONIA AND COCHIN TYPES BY

HARRY SWEETMAN TYPESETTING CORPORATION.

IT WAS PRINTED AND BOUND AT THE PRESS OF

THE WORLD PUBLISHING COMPANY.

DESIGN IS BY LARRY KAMP.